Transition to Palestinian Self-Government: Practical Steps Toward Israeli-Palestinian Peace

Report of a Study Group of
the Middle East Program
Committee on International Security Studies
American Academy of Arts and Sciences
Cambridge, Massachusetts

Ann Mosely Lesch, Principal Author

Published in collaboration with
Indiana University Press
Bloomington and Indianapolis

Contents

Figures

Preface

The report which follows was produced by a Study Group called together by the American Academy of Arts and Sciences through its program on Middle East Security Studies. This program, co-chaired by Philip Khoury of the Massachusetts Institute of Technology and Everett Mendelsohn of Harvard University, is in turn a unit of the Academy's Committee on International Security Studies, chaired by Charles A. Zraket.

The genesis of this report focussing on the "transition period" in the Israeli-Palestinian negotiating process came through a series of conferences involving Israelis, Palestinians (and other Arabs), and Americans held by the Program on Middle East Security Studies at the House of the Academy in Cambridge, Massachusetts and on one occasion in Cairo, Egypt. The intent of these conferences was to focus on the "tough" issues which would be involved in Israeli-Palestinian peacemaking. Four publications were generated by these conferences, each reflecting commissioned studies: "Middle East Security: Two Views," by Ahmad S. Khalidi and Yair Evron (May 1990); "The Palestinian Right of Return: Two Views," by Rashid I. Khalidi and Itamar Rabinovich (October 1990); "Negotiating the Non-Negotiable: Jerusalem in the Framework of an Israeli-Palestinian Settlement," by Naomi Chazan with commentary by Fouad Moughrabi and Rashid I. Khalidi (March 1991); and, "The Saladin Syndrome: Lessons from the Gulf War," by Ze'ev Schiff and Walid Khalidi (August 1991). These papers were published as part of the American Academy's *Emerging Issues Occasional Paper Series* and are available from the Academy.

During the course of the conferences, a number of the participants suggested that we move directly to examining the "realities" of a transition period. The aim would be to de-mystify and to delineate the practical elements and the potential problems which

Israelis and Palestinians would face as they begin to proceed through the several stages of their negotiated settlement.

A joint team of Israelis, Palestinians, and Americans gathered on several occasions to discuss and design such a "transition report." In the summer of 1991, US-based members of the group traveled to Israel, the Occupied Territories, Amman, Cairo, and Tunis. During the course of this trip, discussions were held with individuals across the political spectrum, including officials in government, political activists, and academics in universities and research institutions. The Committee is deeply grateful for the time spent and the views shared by the numerous people who met with the group during its trip.

In addition, the Study Group requested "background memoranda" from a number of individual scholars to help identify critical issues and important questions. The generosity of these colleagues is gratefully acknowledged and the titles of their memoranda are at the end of this Preface.

The realities of actually drafting a text and creating the report were taken on by the US-based members of the group. Throughout the drafting, close consultation and sharing of the text with colleagues in Israel and the Occupied Territories continued.

Mid-way in the drafting process, Ann Lesch was asked by the Study Group to take on the task of preparing the draft and serving as the principal author. She produced successive drafts which were circulated among members of the Study Group, commented upon, and edited by all members of the group and several additional specialists who were called upon for a close reading of specific sections of the text where verification of information was particularly important. A preliminary draft of the Introduction was prepared by Shibley Telhami.

Responsibility for the details of the text lies with the US-based members of the group. The Study Group as a whole endorses the overall themes and the viewpoints developed in the text and noted in the summary. The American Academy of Arts and Sciences is not responsible for any of the points of view adopted in the text.

This report is not a "blueprint" for the transition period nor even recommendations to those engaged in negotiating an agreement between the Israelis and Palestinians. It is, instead, an attempt to identify in direct terms the types of items and issues that will emerge as the processes of self-government are negotiated and developed, with the intent of indicating that the specifics are "doable," non-threatening, and beneficial to both parties. The shape

and form that the specific arrangement for the interim self-government will take is obviously the responsibility of the negotiators
themselves and the parties they represent.

A note on the framework adopted in preparing this report is
important. It became clear early in the planning stages that the
nature of the "final status" agreements would significantly influence
the shape and modalities of the interim period. If ultimate integration of the occupied Palestinian territories into Israel were the final
goal, the interim arrangements would be strikingly different than
if some form of independence or confederation with Jordan was to
be the ultimate outcome. The group consciously chose to work within
the latter framework and thus predicated its study upon this final
outcome. It is obvious to all that only further negotiations will
resolve this point.

The group deeply appreciates the work of the American Academy of Arts and Sciences staff, and especially Annette Mann Bourne,
for continued help throughout the course of the project and for the
final preparation of the manuscript for release. Jeffrey Boutwell,
Associate Executive Officer of the Academy served both as a member
of the Study Group and as coordinator of the project within the
Academy. While the preliminary conferences on issues of Israeli-
Palestinian security were held with the support of the John D. and
Catherine T. MacArthur Foundation, the work involved in the
preparation of the report itself was funded by a grant from the Ford
Foundation.

10 July 1992
Cambridge, Massachusetts

Everett Mendelsohn
Co-Chair
Program on Middle East
Security Studies

Members of the Study Group

Jeffrey Boutwell
American Academy of Arts and Sciences
Cambridge, Massachusetts

Naomi Chazan
Hebrew University
Jerusalem, Israel

Mahdi Abdul Hadi
Palestinian Academic Society
  for the Study of International Affairs
East Jerusalem, West Bank

Ruth Klinov
Hebrew University
Jerusalem, Israel

Ann Lesch
Villanova University
Villanova, Pennsylvania

Everett Mendelsohn
Harvard University
Cambridge, Massachusetts

Fouad Moughrabi
University of Tennessee
Chattanooga, Tennessee

Salim Tamari
Bir Zeit University
Ramallah, West Bank

Shibley Telhami
Cornell University
Ithaca, New York

Mark Tessler
University of Wisconsin-Milwaukee
Milwaukee, Wisconsin

Background Memos for Transition Study Group

Ephraim Ahiram, "Strategy for the Development of Industry in the West Bank and Gaza: A General Framework." (Leonard Davis Institute, Hebrew University, Jerusalem)

Laurie A. Brand, "Palestinians in the Diaspora." (University of Southern California)

Robert O. Freedman, "Soviet Jewish Immigrants and Israel's Next Election." (Baltimore Hebrew University)

Alouph Hareven, "Educational Policies." (Van Leer Institute, Jerusalem)

Edy Kaufman and Mubarak Awad, "Human Rights." (Hebrew University and Nonviolence International)

Baruch Kimmerling, "Achieving a Comprehensive Regional Agreement." (Hebrew University, Jerusalem)

Ruth Klinov, "The Palestinian Economy in Transition" and "Absorption Capacity of the Palestinian State as a Part of a Regional Settlement." (Hebrew University, Jerusalem)

Ann M. Lesch, "Israeli Settlements." (Villanova University)

Moshe Ma'oz, "Toward an Israeli-Palestinian/Arab Settlement." (Hebrew University, Jerusalem)

Khalil Shikaki, "Palestinian Security Requirements and the Political Settlement." (World and Islam Study Enterprise)

Russell A. Stone, "Some Notes on Public Opinion re: An Israeli-Palestinian Settlement." (State University of New York, Buffalo)

Salim Tamari, "Problems of Transition." (Bir Zeit University)

Shibley Telhami, "The Potential Political and Social Stability of a Palestinian State." (Cornell University)

Mark Tessler, "Some Propositions about Democracy in the Arab World and its Relationship to the Israeli-Palestinian Conflict." (University of Wisconsin - Milwaukee)

Elias H. Tuma, "Peace, Economic Cooperation and Integration in the Middle East" and "The Middle East: War, Cease-fire, and After." (University of California, Davis)

Introduction

The initiation of direct negotiations between Israelis, Palestinians, and other Arabs has raised hopes that one of this century's most persistent international problems could finally be settled. This report is intended to build on this hope with substantive suggestions, and also to present some contingency ideas just in case, as so often before, the new hope for progress gives way to despair.

There are two premises in this report. The first is the assumption that the negotiators are limited in their ability to generate substantive ideas by their political constraints and by their strongly-held national and moral claims. If progress is to be made, the negotiations must be pushed away from general principles toward substantive and practical issues; a group of academic experts like this one (made up of Israeli, American, Palestinian, and other Arab scholars) is less constrained in generating such ideas. The second premise is humanitarian: for those who believe that the Israeli-Palestinian status quo, with continued Palestinian and Israeli suffering, is morally unacceptable, there is a need for creative ideas to alleviate the immediate suffering. Even if the current negotiations succeed, most analysts assume that the process will take more time than many suffering local people can afford. These suggestions are therefore made not only to state-actors, but also to individuals and non-governmental organizations who are morally concerned, and who can make some immediate difference even if they cannot affect the direction of the negotiations.

The Practical Considerations

Our starting point is pragmatic. Moral considerations aside, it is clear that the recent momentum in the negotiations is largely due to the fact that all parties have something to gain; the end of the

Cold War between the superpowers, and the war in the Persian Gulf have made this process unavoidable for the key actors in the negotiations.

It is obvious, for example, that, without the active role of the United States, the process could not have begun and is not likely to succeed. While this American role has been made easier by the absence of competition with the Soviet Union, the recent crisis in the Persian Gulf War has made it impossible for the US to ignore the complications that the Arab-Israeli conflict brings to American policy in the Middle East. So long as conflict continues between Israel and its Arab neighbors, the US economic and strategic interests in the Arab world will be difficult to reconcile with the US commitment to the well-being of the state of Israel; only a settlement of the Arab-Israeli conflict can relieve this inherent tension in US interests. Moreover, despite the end of the Cold War, the US cannot disengage itself from the Middle East. Even aside from the obvious interest in oil, the American commitment to Israel, which entails economic, military, and economic support, means that the US is de facto involved.

While the Gulf crisis, at its core, was unrelated to the Arab-Israeli conflict, it is clear that Iraq attempted to exploit this conflict in a way that complicated US policy strategy. And, in October 1990, while the US sought to maintain an international consensus on the Gulf Crisis, Palestinian-Israeli confrontations in Jerusalem nearly derailed the US strategy. As in other Middle East crises of the past, the threat posed by the Arab-Israeli conflict to US interests in the region became impossible to ignore. The American effort to push for a settlement of the Arab-Israeli conflict in the aftermath of the Gulf War is largely driven both by traditional American interests as well as by a new self-image of the United States providing global leadership in the post-Cold War world.

The European states, particularly through their new European Community agencies and through the United Nations, have broadened their interest and active role in Middle East affairs. Enlarging economic ties, coupled with extended political interest, have raised the European stake in the shape of Middle East peacemaking and resulted in their insistence in being included in the current negotiating processes. But it remains clear that, although external parties such as the US and Europe have significant roles to play as supporters and facilitators of the negotiations, it will remain for the negotiating parties of the Middle East to reach agreements and to implement them.

The Palestinian interest in moving forward is obvious: the status quo is wholly unacceptable, and, if the past is any indication, time has only made the Palestinian predicament more difficult. The Gulf War created new Palestinian refugees from Kuwait, decreased funds available to Palestinian communities, and weakened the leverage of Palestinian allies. Any promise of reversing Palestinian fortunes is welcome.

Most Arab states also have interest in making immediate progress on the Arab-Israeli conflict. Those Arab states who joined the US-led alliance against Iraq have to show something for this support. Most, especially Egypt and Syria, had promised their confused populations that their behavior would lead to settling the Arab-Israeli conflict after the Gulf war. The immediate quiet in the region following the war is due in part to the rising hope about the prospect of Arab-Israeli peace.

The need for Arab states to see a settlement of the Palestinian-Israeli conflict is deeply rooted in the nature of Middle East politics. While most Arab governments continue to face transnational challenges to their legitimacy, the Israeli-Palestinian conflict has remained as one of the key issues fueling transnationalism in the region. Settling this conflict could substantially erode the appeal of Arab transnational movements.

Israel, too, has much to gain. Quite clearly, Israel emerged in a superior strategic position with the destruction of Iraq's military potential, and the absence of the Soviet Union as a patron of Arab enemies further eroded the threat of an Arab military coalition confronting Israel. Yet, the Iraqi Scud attacks brought home the need for an end to the state of war with Arab states. Moreover, the economic costs of absorbing hundreds of thousands of Soviet Jewish immigrants showed the need to cut high Israeli military expenditure; and the continued occupation of the West Bank and Gaza had negative implications economically, diplomatically and militarily. With the election in June 1992 of a Labor government led by Yitzhak Rabin, Israel is poised to take advantage of a very favorable regional and international configuration with which to make peace.

In short, all sides have immediate interests in making progress, but substantial disagreements remain on the nature of a settlement, and domestic political considerations within each polity make progress especially difficult.

Figure 1
Israel and the Occupied Territories

Human Considerations

Aside from the obvious motivations of coinciding interests (which led our group of Arabs, Israelis and Americans to agree on some broad outlines of a settlement), there are also compelling humanitarian reasons to actively seek a settlement to the Israeli-Palestinian conflict.

On the Palestinian side, conditions of occupation are hard to bear. Under occupation, Palestinians have no civil rights, can be arrested without charges, have substantial economic and political constraints, and live in perpetual uncertainty about the future. While it is easy to rationalize measures of occupation as necessary for security and maintenance of law and order, these measures were always understood to be temporary. Yet, for the Palestinians, occupation is not a temporary exception to the rule but a lasting way of life; a significant majority of Palestinians in the West Bank and Gaza have been born or raised under occupation and do not know another way of life.

For the Israelis, occupation has not brought a sense of security. Attacks on Israeli soldiers and civilians continue; the economic costs of occupation increasingly divert needed funds from pressing domestic needs; the presence of large numbers of Palestinians under Israeli control poses a challenge to Israel's Jewish identity on the one hand and to its democratic character on the other. And the absence of Palestinian-Israeli agreement has been a barrier to concluding peace treaties with Arab states that could accommodate Israel's security needs.

The compelling needs of the Palestinian and the Israeli people are immediate and should be addressed even independently from the peace negotiations. In this regard, international agencies, non-governmental organizations, and concerned individuals have a role to play. Our report makes some specific recommendations on this issue.

Symmetries and Asymmetries

No progress can be made without concessions by all sides. And neither the Palestinians nor the Israelis have a monopoly on human suffering. Still, it is very important to note that there are serious asymmetries between the parties that require parallel asymmetries in the initial concessions to be made. For example, while all sides have legitimate security requirements, Israeli security requirements seem more dramatic for reasons of its small size and its history of continued conflict with the Arab states. This entails that a realistic settlement may require some asymmetrical concessions favoring Israel: the degree of demilitarization, the inclusion of buffer zones, and the types of arms-control agreements that emerge, especially in relation to weapons of mass destruction, must all take this asymmetry into account.

Similarly, the suffering of the Palestinians, and the basic disadvantages inherent in occupation entail that many of the early concessions pertaining to economic assistance, territorial compromise, human rights and the building of autonomous institutions will favor the Palestinians. It is therefore important to keep in mind while reading this report that our focus is primarily on economic and political issues, over which Palestinians and Israelis have many commonalities of interests, even if those are asymmetrical. It is also important to note that the examination of security issues in this report is preliminary and is intended to address only those broad requirements that pertain to the political and economic questions; in the end, it is impossible to separate these issues. However, the American Academy believes that security issues are so important to ending the conflict and securing a just and stable peace that a separate study group is preparing another report that focusses on security in much greater detail. The advantages to Israel should become even more obvious in that report.

The Context of the Proposals

The organization of this report is straightforward. Suggestions of immediate action to alleviate local suffering come first; these suggestions apply whether or not the negotiations move successfully ahead. Next come suggestions about the nature of the transitional period which cannot be made without reference to a targeted final settlement. Since these suggestions are central to this report, it is important to note the context in which they are made. First, both Palestinians and Israelis have agreed that there must be a transitional period preceding a final settlement which will be the focus of the first stage of negotiations. Second, the suggestions in this report do not constitute "blueprints" for a settlement. The ideas presented are made in order to help start a substantive debate of the issues. Third, since any transitional arrangements must make a final settlement more realizable, it is important to discuss the principles and potential shape of a final settlement. Even if this study group did not have a preference for one form of final settlement, the transitional proposals would have been largely the same: since the negotiations are based on United Nations Security Council resolution 242, which calls for the exchange of territory for peace, and since one of the possible outcomes to be negotiated is a Palestinian state, any transitional period must leave this option open in future negotiations. Yet, if Israel and the Palestinians agree on this option as a final settlement, it can only be implemented if the transitional arrangements create more autonomous Palestinian economic and political institutions than now exist under Israeli occupation.

Our recommendations pertaining to the transitional stage are thus somewhat independent from the final settlement; they are intended not to rule out any option, including the possibility of a Palestinian state. But we do have preferences for a final settlement; we cannot foresee an end to the Arab-Israeli conflict if Israel continues to control the West Bank and Gaza. And we believe that the most stable end-result is Palestinian self-determination.

Our reasoning is not primarily moral preference but, ultimately, pragmatic. At its core, the Israeli-Palestinian conflict involves both territory and the problem of nationalism in a world of nation-states. The tragedy of the Palestinian-Israeli conflict is that, because each has suffered from the national aspirations of the other, both have overlooked the striking similarities in the rise of their legitimate national movements.

Neither Jews nor Palestinians sought nationalism as an ideal end. Many of the Zionists in nineteenth-century Europe were egalitarian universalists who sought full and equal citizenship in a Europe that advocated these same ideals. But the rise of geographic and ethnic nationalism, and the prevalence of anti-semitism, made their dream impossible, their ideal unattainable. These Jewish intellectuals, persecuted and excluded because of their Jewish ethnicity, awoke to an uncompromising reality: in a world of nationalism, one can attain relative normality only by having one's own nationalism manifesting itself in one's own homeland. Nationalism was thus, not an ideal, but the necessary compromise with a non-egalitarian world of nationalism.

Many Palestinians, having suffered the consequences of Zionism, have found it difficult to accept the reality and the legitimacy of Jewish national aspirations — the fact that Jewish identity, for the Jews, is not merely religious and ethnic. But so too have many Israelis failed to recognize the national aspirations of the Palestinian people, despite the many similarities in the rise of Zionism and Palestinian nationalism.

18

Palestinians made homeless by the conflict with Israel in 1948 initially fought, not only for their distinct national identity but also for justice, for the right to return to their homes, and for broader Arab ideals. But several decades of continued conflict and suffering have taught the Palestinians a lesson that Jews learned a century ago. Despite an international rhetoric of justice, and a regional rhetoric of Arab solidarity, the world in which they live is a world of nation-states. Whereas states like Syria and Egypt professed Arab and Islamic objectives, the interests of their nation-states always came first. Palestinians on the other hand, like their Jewish counterparts, learned that, ideals aside, relative normality in a world of nation-states can only be attained by having one's own nationality reflecting itself in one's own national homeland.

The rise of Palestinian nationalism has, ironically, opened the way for Israeli-Palestinian reconciliation. While implementing the literal return of Palestinians to their homes within Israel is incompatible with Israel as a Jewish state, Palestinian nationalism, if actuated in a national homeland in part of Palestine (the West Bank and Gaza), can coexist with the Jewish state of Israel.

If the Israeli-Palestinian conflict has taught us anything it is this: one cannot solve the national problem of one people by creating a national problem for another. Jordan cannot become the national homeland of the Palestinians, even if half of the Jordanian population may be ethnically Palestinian; what will become of the national aspirations of the Jordanian half? Whether or not Jordanian nationalism (or, for that matter, Palestinian, Kuwaiti, Lebanese, or Israeli nationalism) existed before the twentieth century is strictly irrelevant, as nation-states in the region have become an inescapable reality today. Both Palestinian and Jordanian nationalism must be recognized. Similarly, the reality of Zionism as a Jewish national movement makes it impossible to contemplate an option which does not leave Israel as a state with a Jewish majority.

For those who ultimately seek more egalitarian solutions, our more limited recommendations offer some hope. Recognition, legitimacy, and acceptance may appear merely symbolic, but they are much more. Only after Palestinians and Israelis accept the national legitimacy of each other can both sides hope to transcend their national dilemmas. It is with the pragmatic recognition of these historical dilemmas that our suggestions about the shape of a final settlement are made.

I

Civic and Political Institutions

A key unfulfilled expectation of the Egyptian-Israeli Peace Treaty was the establishment of a transition period of interim self-government for the Palestinians. The negotiations concerning Palestinian self-rule lasted for over two years following the signing of the treaty in 1979. Although the Israeli and Egyptian proposals differed, both accepted the principle of a Palestinian Self-Governing Authority. Indeed in its proposal of January 1982 Israel took credit for first raising the idea of substantial "autonomy" for the Palestinians of the occupied territories. Neither the Jordanians nor the Palestinians joined the negotiations, which were effectively dead by the time Israel invaded Lebanon in June 1982. At present Israel and the Palestinians are, for the first time, negotiating directly on the terms of self-governance. The ideas presented below explore the nature of possible civic and political institutions as a means of indicating what may be necessary and achievable.[1]

The development and consolidation during the transition period of structures of governance by Palestinians is essential, both to begin the process of creating viable Palestinian institutions in the future and to lay the foundation for a new set of political relationships in the region. In the short run, civic and political institutions are needed for Palestinians to cope with the difficulties of daily life and to reduce dependence on Israel. In the slightly longer run, they will underpin the interim period as occupation is withdrawn and determine the direction and key elements of the long-range situation, whether the Palestinians gain an independent state in the West Bank and Gaza Strip or a confederation with Jordan. These institutional forms will also improve the nature of Israeli-Palestinian relations as the occupation recedes and is superceded by a relationship based on mutuality and equality.

Palestinians themselves emphasize the need both to strengthen existing institutions and to develop new structures of governance. Israel's Likud government which began the negotiations indicated that, during the anticipated period of self-rule, the Palestinians would administer significant areas of social and economic life. Even though their position would severely limit Palestinian central policy-making authority, then Prime Minister Yitzhak Shamir has stated: "they will have all the prerogatives of a state, aside from an army and foreign policy."[2] The interim plan advanced in 1982 by then Prime Minister Menachem Begin did call for a region-wide Administrative Council with some real authority. Israel's new Prime Minister Yitzhak Rabin indicates that he would accept far-reaching self-rule for Palestinians, including a virtual freeze on new settlements.[3] As this report goes to press the negotiations re-open with a new Israeli negotiating team committed to reaching a self-rule agreement in no more than nine to twelve months.

The Status Quo

The Military Government in the Occupied Territories

Following their military victory over Jordan, Syria and Egypt in June 1967, the Israeli armed forces established military rule throughout the Occupied Territories (OT). As expressed in Proclamation #1, the commanding officers were "responsible for security and the maintenance of public order."[4] Proclamation #2 vested "all powers of government, legislature, appointment and administration in relation to the Region or its inhabitants" in the military governor, who was appointed by the Chief of Staff of the Israeli Defense Forces (IDF) and subordinate to the General Headquarters' Coordinator of Territories. The regional command for the West Bank (later renamed Judea and Samaria) was located in Beit-El, north of Ramallah, and the regional command for the Gaza Strip and Northern Sinai was located in Gaza city. The military governor could delegate aspects of his authority to district military commanders and to senior staff in the headquarters, notably the Internal Affairs Officer in the Regional Command. The West Bank was divided into six military districts, each headed by a military governor. Legal staff came from the Military Advocate General's Corps and staff responsible for economic and social issues could be seconded from the respective ministries; the sections for Economic Affairs, and Administration and Services were particularly important.

Subsequent military orders retained pre-occupation Jordanian and Egyptian laws in the respective territories but stated "each security enactment has preference over any local laws, even if it has not explicitly repealed the same." During the quarter century of Israeli rule, over 1300 military orders have been issued that have radically altered the legal status of the OT. Moreover, in November 1981, a Civil Administration was introduced (see Figure 2) and subsequently, the IDF regional command controlled security issues while the civil administration handled social and economic affairs; nonetheless, executive, legislative and judicial power remain concentrated in the hands of the military commanders.[5] Because of this change Palestinians were required to turn to the civil administration for non-security matters. The new system appeared designed to pave the way for strong Israeli control of the autonomy regime. This matched Prime Minister Begin's claim that he would never relinquish sovereignty over the West Bank.

The military government kept the basic administrative apparatus of the preexisting systems. Palestinian staff were retained in the departments of agriculture, communication (postal and telephone services), transport, education, health, public works and social affairs; some Palestinians worked in customs and taxation, but none in the prison system. Local courts functioned under the supervision of the Israeli Ministry of Justice, but the military government had to appoint substantial numbers of new policemen, since most had fled from the West Bank to Jordan (see discussion in Section II). Israeli officers retained the power of approval in the Palestinian-staffed departments.[6] The military government hired and fired Palestinian staff, controlled the departmental budgets, and set policy. The impact is shown in the following examples:

• **Education:** The government sector comprises 77 percent of West Bank schools and 40 percent of Gaza Strip schools. (See below on UNRWA schools.) The Palestinian director of education in each district handles minor technical or personnel issues, but the military-appointed officer of education, with an Israeli staff, makes key decisions on hiring and firing teachers, structuring the curricula, selecting textbooks, instituting new programs or deleting existing courses, constructing new schools, and holding in-service courses for teachers.[7] As a result, no West Bank school employed a full-time librarian or laboratory technician after 1976; physical education, arts and home economics courses were dropped in many schools; no public school teacher had been sent

Figure 2

Organizational Chart - Gaza Strip

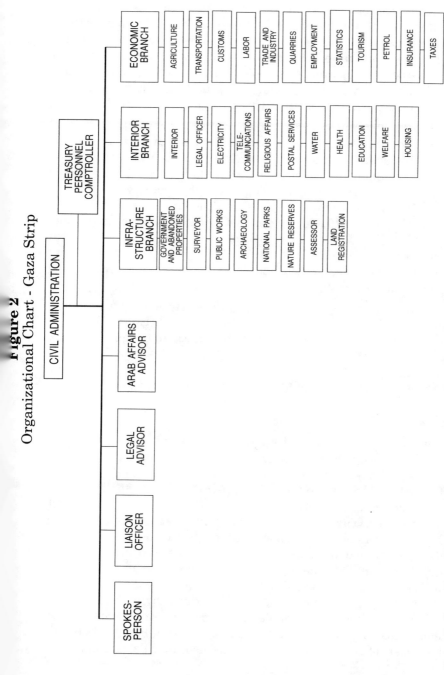

Source: Sara Roy, *The Gaza Strip Survey* (Jerusalem: The West Bank Database Project, 1986) p. 128.

to study abroad on a scholarship as of 1982; there was a dearth of in-service training courses for teachers; no government schools were expanded or built without external funding; and the pupil-teacher ratio deteriorated, with nearly fifty students per classroom in government schools in the Gaza Strip. Even though education is compulsory through the ninth grade, a third of the eligible students do not attend junior high school in the Gaza Strip.

• **Health:** The military government spent $30 per capita on medical services in 1986 in the OT as against $350 per capita in Israel. The 1985 budget for all nine government hospitals in the West Bank was $5 million, and government hospitals could not hire additional physicians, even though unemployed physicians were eager to work and even though the physician/population ratio in 1986 for the OT was 8/10,000 in contrast to 28/10,000 in Israel and 22/10,000 in Jordan. In the Gaza Strip, the three government hospitals have only 586 beds (1990) and yet the military government prevented the Red Crescent Society from constructing a new hospital.[8]

The quality of administrative services deteriorated further during the Palestinian *intifada* (uprising), which began in December 1987. Palestinian police and most tax collectors resigned, and the government reduced funding to most departments. The Palestinian staff already lacked authority to make substantive decisions; subsequently, they lacked funds to maintain minimal services.

Changes from Pre-War Situation

Jerusalem: On 27 June 1967 Israel annexed the east side of the city (previously under Jordanian control), and extended the municipal boundaries north to Qalandiya airport and south almost to Bethlehem. Israeli law and administration were applied to the enlarged area, which was placed under the authority of the Israeli municipality. The Jordanian municipality was disbanded and its Palestinian mayor was deported that fall. In August 1980, Israel declared unified Jerusalem the eternal capital of Israel. Palestinians living in Jerusalem have been in an anomalous legal and political situation: not subject to some of the constraints imposed by the military government and yet constricted by a ring of Israeli urban settlements and unable to take control over their socio-economic life. They were given the option of taking Israeli citizenship but most refused not wanting to relinquish their Palestinian political identity. Israel treats them as non-citizen residents of Israel. In principle they have access to the various social services given to Israeli Jews and are governed by Israeli civil law rather than the military law of the OT. Since the Gulf war, Israel has attempted to sever ties between East Jerusalem and the West Bank by curtailing access to the city. That has hampered the normally intense religious, cultural, social, educational and trade relations between Jerusalem and the surrounding region.

District Commissioner in the West Bank: The Israeli military governor abolished the position of district commissioner and assumed his powers.[9] That official had provided a link between the central government in Amman (which had annexed the West Bank in 1950) and the municipal and rural councils. Local branches of government departments were under his authority. The District Committee for Planning was also abolished; its functions were assumed by the Supreme Planning Council of the Military Government, an all-Israeli body.

Legislative Council in the Gaza Strip: The Gaza Strip had been ruled by an Egyptian governor general, appointed by the Egyptian president, as occupied territory held by Egyptian forces on behalf of the Palestinians; Egypt never annexed Gaza. The governor chaired an executive council and appointed all administrative officials, most of whom were Palestinian. In 1960 elections were held for the National Union, the one political party, and in 1962 a half-elected Legislative Council was formed, having limited powers. In 1967 the Israeli military governor assumed the powers of the Egyptian governor general, abolished the Legislative Council, and banned the National Union.

Israeli settlements: Since 1967 at least 130 settlements have been built on the West Bank with over 100,000 residents; 18 settlements in the Gaza Strip have 5,000 residents, and eight large settlement-neighborhoods have been built in expanded Jerusalem with 120,000 residents. The approximately 225,000 Israeli settlers contrast with at least two million Palestinian residents. Nonetheless, half of the land has been seized for the use of settlements and the armed forces. Moreover, in 1991 construction more than doubled: 14,650 homes were built and 14 new communities established, an increase of 60 percent in housing in one year.[10] The settlements have municipal councils and courts, as an extension of Israeli municipal law. Religious courts also function in the settlements, to handle personal status issues. Five regional councils were established in 1979, based on Israeli district law, which have wide jurisdiction over OT territory (see economics section for a discussion of land expropriation). The settlement areas are extraterritorial enclaves in the OT, and the residents are not subject to the same laws as the Palestinian residents, living in contiguous areas.

Quasi-Independent Institutions

Certain indigenous institutions continued to operate after 1967, with altered status. Those included municipal councils, rural councils, and chambers of commerce. The UN Relief and Works Agency (UNRWA) also maintained its educational, health and welfare programs in the refugee camps. Charitable societies, private schools and universities, unions and cooperatives also have continued to exist. They function under limitations imposed by the military government, for example:

Municipal Councils: Municipal councils had authority over planning, building, business-licensing, health, sanitation, sewage, fire brigades, operating public markets and slaughter houses, and schools within municipal boundaries.[11] Their powers eroded substantially, since the Interior Affairs Officer in the Military Government had to approve their budget, fix tax rates and approve any changes in the municipal by-laws. Moreover, the Military Government could exert leverage over the municipalities by withholding financial support (loans, development funds, tax rebates) and denying permits and licenses to residents. Municipalities were not allowed to purchase spare parts for or replace electricity generators, and the above-mentioned Israeli Supreme Planning Council can amend and revoke municipalities' plans and licenses.

The 25 West Bank towns, whose jurisdiction covers 40 percent of the region's population, were due to hold elections in August 1967, but the military government postponed them until 1972. In 1976, after the four-year terms expired, a second set of elections were held this time with pro-PLO figures running and capturing most of the mayoral offices. A military order in December 1977 suspended further elections indefinitely. In 1982, the members of most municipal councils were fired when they refused to cooperate with the new Israeli Civil Administrator; even the appointed Gaza City municipal council was removed from office. (The Gaza Strip has four appointed municipal councils, regulated according to the municipal law of 1934; the last election in Gaza City was held in 1946, during the British mandate.) Israeli military officers subsequently ran the towns directly, thereby removing an important buffer between the residents and the military government. Some Palestinians did agree to accept appointments in the late 1980s in an effort to ease the tensions and improve municipal services. A foreign development expert, Lance Matteson, argues that services have deteriorated in the military-run towns and the remaining municipalities have been frequently "denied their legal fiscal share of tax revenues... [and] increasingly prevented from exercising their legal authority to issue building permits within their borders."[12]

Village Councils: Most of the 96 village councils on the West Bank stopped functioning in 1967, but 85 were subsequently reactivated, with the military government (later, the civil administration) assuming the supervisory authority previously held by the Jordanian District Commissioner.[13] The councils' authority is more limited than municipal councils. Elections were held in 60 villages in the West Bank in 1975, under the auspices of the Internal Affairs Officer of the Military Government, but a military order in December 1977 suspended further elections indefinitely and the number of village councils dropped to 75 in the mid-eighties. The Gaza Strip has eight appointed village councils. Moreover, at least 300 villages lack any village council and are regulated by a government-appointed *mukhtar* (headman), who monitors internal security, passes on directives from the military government, and authenticates documents for which he receives a fee.

Chambers of Commerce: These local bodies perform important services by representing the interests of merchants, processing documents needed by ministries in Amman, and certifying produce for export to Jordan. The military governor suspended elections for their administrative councils, due in 1969 after a four year term, and placed them under the supervision of the head of the economic branch of the regional command (later under the civil administration). Elections were held in four towns in 1972-3, in part because some councils no longer had a quorum; but the above-mentioned military order in 1977 suspended elections indefinitely. Israel recently allowed six chambers to hold elections in 1991-2. Several chambers of commerce, however, have not elected new administrative councils in a quarter century. Not until 1989 did the chambers found a federation, the first time an OT-level body could represent business interests.[14]

Labor Unions: Labor unions were active in the West Bank and Gaza Strip prior to the Israeli occupation.[15] The military government allowed unions to continue functioning in the West Bank but closed the Gaza labor federation and its six affiliates. When allowed to reopen in 1980, the unions in Gaza could only re-enroll their pre-1967 members and could not hold elections. Nonetheless, three affiliates held illegal elections in spring 1987, which resulted in military raids on their premises and the arrest of officers. Although West Bank unions were not allowed to open new branches or to operate in East Jerusalem, they managed to expand rapidly in the 1980s and provide increasingly significant social services for their members, including laborers in Israel. Hampered by frequent arrest of union leaders and split by political differences, the rival labor federations nevertheless partially reunited in 1990 in the face of the challenges of the intifada. Professional associations function (and hold internal elections) in both the West Bank and Gaza, including journalists, writers, artists, doctors, dentists, lawyers, and engineers; but they lack formal authority to maintain professional standards and represent group interests.

Private Universities: Six universities have been established in the OT, of which only one pre-dated the occupation.[16] The incentive to open universities came in part from the difficulties students faced in leaving the OT to attend universities in the Arab states. Local universities found it difficult to operate, given the censorship of imported books, high taxes on imported laboratory and audiovisual equipment, and restrictions on work permits for faculty. In 1980, military order #854 shifted control over the universities from their own boards of trustees to the Military Government, virtually removing any distinction between universities and elementary and secondary institutes. Although not fully implemented due to strong Palestinian and international objections, the Military Government education officer (later connected to the civil administration) acquired the authority to license each university on an annual basis, issue faculty permits for only 45 days (rather than an academic year), regulate permits for residents of Gaza or Jerusalem to teach in the West Bank, and control the creation of additional departments or colleges in the universities. Najah University's request in 1980 to open a college of agriculture was denied until 1986 and Bethlehem University's programs in hotel management, nursing and social work were hampered in their operations. In February 1988, all the universities were closed on the basis of three-month (renewable) orders from the military government; in late spring 1992, Bir Zeit University was the last of the OT universities allowed to reopen.

UNRWA: The UN has operated the 19 refugee camps in the West Bank and 8 camps in the Gaza Strip since 1949-50.[17] At most twelve percent of the West Bank population lives in those camps, which average 5-6,000 persons, whereas 55 percent of the Gaza Strip population lives in camps, averaging 32-33,000 persons. Each camp has a Palestinian director, who supervises the maintenance, health, education, and welfare services, including food aid, which are all operated by refugees. UNRWA primary and junior high schools comprise nine per cent of West Bank schools and half of the Gaza Strip schools. UNRWA also operates four post-secondary teacher training and vocational schools, one (now partly coeducational) in Gaza and three on the West Bank, including one for women. UNRWA cannot shield the camp residents from raids by the army or security forces, from prolonged curfews or from the demolition of houses. (See security section on UNRWA protection efforts.) UNRWA is viewed as necessary by Palestinians, but also anomalous; although only fifteen international staff work in UNRWA offices in the OT, these tend to be the most senior officials. Moreover, policy is set in the headquarters in Vienna and coordination is required with several UN agencies, including UNICEF for health, water and preschool education, UNESCO for education, and WHO for medical staff. Thus, UNRWA priorities and practices may diverge from the educational and social directions being promoted by Palestinian residents.

Restrictions on Institutional Development

The occupation has restricted the Palestinians' ability to function politically, much less lay an institutional foundation for eventual self-government. The military government limits freedom of speech, publishing, organizing or meeting; bans public political gatherings; and censors newspapers and other publications. Daily newspapers are published only in East Jerusalem, which falls under the less restrictive Israeli law; nonetheless, the Israeli censor reviews all their materials, often deleting controversial items, and newspaper distribution is frequently banned in the West Bank and Gaza Strip even while permitted in Jerusalem and the Arab towns of Israel. Political life is forced underground or expressed through the indirect channels noted above. Since political activities are illegal, people can be charged with a "security" violation for even having the Palestinian flag in their homes.

Institutional development is also constricted, as Matteson notes,[18] since the Israeli government has "refused...to register Palestinian institutions, closed them by military order, prohibited whole classes of them outright, neutralized their leadership (by arrest, deposing, deportation, harassment, threats, etc.), restricted or blocked member[ship] applicants, blocked or restricted elections or meetings,... delayed or blocked movement of their capital, censored or prohibited gathering or publication of their technical information, and destroyed or appropriated their property." The organizations affected range across a wide spectrum: not only municipalities, village councils, and unions but also educational and research institutes, corporate bodies, unions and cooperatives, and charitable or non-profit institutions. Matteson adds that civic life is further constricted since Palestinian civil servants are banned from coordinating with colleagues in the private sector: government teachers and social workers, for example, are not allowed to collaborate formally with their counterparts in private institutions. He concludes: "the total negation of Palestinian national public institutions constitutes perhaps the single largest external constraint on Palestinian development."

Palestinians must obtain permissions and licenses from the Israeli authorities in order to carry out even the most simple social and economic activities. Requests for permits are often denied or left unanswered, giving Palestinians no choice but to act without Israeli approval and thereby making them additionally vulnerable to Israeli interference in their daily lives. New restrictions in place since 1991 on access from the West Bank to Jerusalem have further disrupted daily life, since the principal hospitals, schools, social and charitable services, and communications outlets are located there. The Palestinians thus exist in a situation of fundamental insecurity, lacking any recourse when officials block their projects or thwart their socio-economic development efforts.

While this situation causes hardship and provides occupation authorities with mechanisms to control Palestinian society, an equally serious consequence is the inability of Palestinians to implement plans, coordinate the development of their communities, and establish or maintain the civic institutions required for eventual self-government.

Palestinian Political and Civic Activities

Despite these restrictions, Palestinian political life has evolved substantially since the occupation began.[19] At first, residents thought that the occupation would be as brief as Israel's rule over

Gaza had been in 1956-57. The urban elites protested the annexation of Jerusalem to Israel and refused to accept changes in the educational and legal systems. Demonstrations and strikes on the West Bank resulted in widespread arrests and deportations; a full-scale insurrection in the Gaza Strip was crushed in 1970-71. From 1973 to 1977, the Palestine National Front (PNF) grouped several underground political organizations and organized the national blocs that successfully contested the 1976 municipal elections. When the mayors expressed nationalist views and criticized the occupation, the military government began to restrict their activities and cracked down on the PNF. Then the National Guidance Committee, a publicly known body consisting of leading mayors and professionals, attempted to coordinate protests against the autonomy plan outlined in the Camp David negotiations among Israel, Egypt and the United States. The government banned the Guidance Committee in 1982 at the same time that it closed down most of the municipalities.

Subsequently, the only outlets for organized Palestinian activity became the chambers of commerce, charitable societies, professional and trade unions, and grassroots organizations. The latter became important during the 1980s as clandestine political groups established competing structures to provide health services and meet the needs of women and youths.[20] They addressed problems in the neglected rural areas as well as the towns and camps, and provided a means to mobilize deprived elements in the community. Young people who participated in voluntary work groups or in student councils at the universities became activists as adults in the medical, agricultural, and women's spheres. Medical committees became particularly active, establishing health clinics in villages, promoting preventive medicine and improved sanitation, and teaching first-aid and hygiene.[21] Those efforts also contributed to weakening the traditional political elite, whose political power had already been diminished by the closure of municipalities and whose patron-client relationships had been weakened by changes in economic patterns and the social mobilization of disadvantaged groups.

Those structures formed the underpinning for the *intifada* that began in December 1987, and that sought to create alternative governing structures. The intifada also represented a significant attempt to distance the Palestinians from Israeli authority. The Unified National Leadership of the Uprising (UNLU) tried to avoid problems that political groups had faced in the past: its members remained anonymous, in part so arrest would not decapitate the

31

movement, but especially to emphasize the primacy of the grass-roots community action and diminish the stress on individual leaders. Even though the local committees were banned in mid-1988, neighborhood groups and the network of grassroots organizations maintained the momentum of the uprising. After the Gulf war in 1991, these committees became the primary networks for economic and social development in the territories.

The Palestinian situation was harmed by the crisis in the Gulf, which polarized the Arab world.[22] Some Palestinians in the OT began to worry that in-fighting among political factions was hurting the Palestinians themselves (for recent security concerns, see Section II.) They were also concerned that the grassroots institutions and mass organizations remained rudimentary, and that a higher degree of coordination was required. Such coordination already existed through the federation of chambers of commerce, formed in 1989, and among the universities, whose Council for Higher Education was established in 1978. That Council helped to maintain a degree of coordination among the academic programs in the absence of a Palestinian ministry of education. The four women's committees affiliated with different political groups maintained contact through a coordinating committee. But similar coordinating efforts had failed among the four groups operating in the field of community medicine and the trade union movement only managed to bring three of its four political trends into a reunited federation in the West Bank. This resulted in damaging competition and even duplication of medical and trade union services. OT-wide councils in agriculture, housing, industry and tourism could, in theory, increase the cost-efficiency of services, reduce competition and duplication, and promote professionalism. However, they could also lead to overcentralization, control by a dominant political faction, and the stifling of local initiatives and spontaneity.

An effort was made in mid-1991 to form such coordinating councils, with the West Bank and Gaza Strip represented on a 2:1 basis (see economics section for details). But many remained skeptical of their value, since they seemed to promote control by Fatah, the leading political group in the PLO; since representation was on the basis of faction, they could become a new arena for political struggle minimizing the role of independents and professionals. The move from the anonymous UNLU to public membership in councils, elections to chambers of commerce, and the high-profile delegation for negotiations emphasizes a return to traditional politics, based on personages, factions, clans, and regions. Nonetheless, the councils have the potential to initiate a process of planning and controlling economic resources, and potentially to serve as a foundation for functional administrative bodies run by Palestinians. Conversely, if Israel chose to suppress them, their public nature would place them at risk, as mayors and above-ground committees were exposed in the past.

Negotiating Phase

Progress toward peace requires that constraints on political and civic life be diminished and the construction and enhancement of Palestinian institutions be accelerated. Then Palestinians would be able to address community needs and prepare for self-rule and, of equal importance, strengthen the commitment to the negotiating process. There has been a slight opening in the restrictive policies of the military government — shown in the elections for some chambers of commerce, reopening of the universities, and tacit toleration of the new coordinating councils — which provides slightly greater space in which Palestinians can operate. But no basic shifts in the structure of Israeli policy have occurred that would enable the Palestinian institutions to acquire significant independence in their operational spheres. Some within Israel have advocated significant liberalization of occupation practice as a means of strengthening Palestinian social and economic life independent of the negotiating process.

Differing Positions

Nonetheless, with the beginning of formal bilateral and multilateral negotiations, the institutional developments necessary for Palestinians to govern themselves have been accepted by Israel as a legitimate subject for political bargaining. Israel has expressed willingness to devolve authority over certain administrative, economic and service areas to the Palestinian community,[23] for which departments in the military government already exist and which are partly or largely staffed by Palestinians; these include: justice, personnel matters, agriculture and fisheries, education, culture and sports, budget and taxation, health, industry, commerce and tourism, labor and social welfare, local police, local courts, and prisons for non-security offenses, local transport and communications, municipal affairs, and religious affairs.

That list omits several functions, including regional planning, public works, internal affairs, electricity, water and land. It does not provide for the establishment of an OT-wide administration to coordinate the sectors, much less an elected authority. Use of the words "management" and "supervision" imply that power to make policy might be restricted. All foreign policy and internal and external security would remain in Israel's hands, although public order would be maintained in cooperation with the local police. Israeli settlers would be excluded from the purview of the Palestinian administrative bodies. Such a system would relieve Israel of the burden of operating schools and hospitals and continue recent trends toward loosening economic restrictions, while keeping ultimate control in its hands.

The principles underlying the Palestinian negotiating position are based on the PNC peace initiative of November 1988, which calls for the establishment of a Palestinian state on the basis of the concept of partition (UNGA Resolution 181 of 1947) in the territories of the West Bank and the Gaza Strip, including East Jerusalem. The Palestinians seek elections for a 180-member legislative assembly in the OT, to which a 20-member executive council would be responsible. The self-governing authority would have executive, legislative and judicial powers, and the military government would be abolished. The authority of the self-governing entity would derive from elections by the Palestinian people, not from an outside source. All "powers, responsibilities and jurisdictions"[24] controlled by the Israeli military government would be transferred to the Palestinian legislature, including control over water and land. Israeli troops would withdraw from populated Arab areas and internal security would be maintained by a "strong Palestinian law enforcement force" together with UN peace-keeping troops. Only foreign affairs and external defense would remain under Israeli authority. The Palestinian delegation also calls for the immediate halt to constructing settlements and measures to uphold human rights in the OT.

Despite the significant gap, there is some common ground between the Israeli route to administrative autonomy and the early stages of the Palestinian route to independence, so far as institutions and structures of governance are concerned. The negotiations will test the limits that are possible in attaining self-rule and establish the process by which authority will be gradually transferred from Israel to the Palestinian entity. For this set of negotiations the Palestinians accepted a number of significant limitations including restricting the agenda to discussion of the transition period and interim self-government.

Political Measures

During the negotiations, Israel could take several important steps that would facilitate the peace process. (Other measures are suggested under Security and Economy.) These include:

- **Political gatherings to discuss the negotiating options**. Some assemblies were permitted after the Madrid conference, but were labeled informational meetings in which the delegates would explain their negotiating strategy and listen to the perspectives and grievances of the public. A wider range of political meetings with fewer restrictions could be allowed.

- **Reporting and analysis of political issues**. Newspapers and journals should be free to write articles, op-eds and editorials debating political issues without submitting them to the censor for prior approval. The newspapers should circulate in the OT without interference. Fostering a free discussion would encourage Palestinians to search for constructive solutions.

- **Reduced restrictions on civic life**. Professional and labor unions could be given greater freedom to recruit members, expand their authority, and plan for internal elections where needed. Charitable societies could be permitted to receive unrestricted contributions and to operate without security surveillance. Private universities could be encouraged to function freely and to expand their planning efforts in anticipation of the needs of the interim phase.

- **Palestinian political committees to provide links between the delegation and the public**. Such committees were initiated after the Madrid conference, but their members risk arrest or deportation. Understandings should be given that participation would not be considered a hostile act by the security forces but would be welcomed as efforts supportive of a negotiated solution. Moreover, Palestinian participants would need to come from a range of political groups and include independents, in order to have legitimacy and local support.

- **Reinvigorated construction of coordinating councils.** Palestinians could work to ensure that the OT-wide councils include representatives of not only political factions but of independents and professionals and that they are not operated as the arm of one group, in order to maintain community support and avoid overcentralization. Meanwhile, local-level groups should seek to reduce their duplication and competition and at least informally coordinate their provision of services and training to the communities.

- **Resumption of local level elections.** The elections to chambers of commerce could continue, with Israel agreeing to not place restrictions on the persons who can run for office. Long overdue elections to municipal and village councils might be held in the latter stage of negotiations, as a gesture of goodwill that would encourage a peace accord and formalize local centers of authority having tangible benefit for the residents. These elections should not be seen as a substitute for an OT-wide self-rule authority, but they could be welcomed in the context of a negotiated accord.[25] If municipal council elections do occur, the Palestinians are likely to call for international observers, in part for the practical value of helping to ensure fair elections and in part for the symbolic value of asserting a legitimate international presence vis-a-vis the OT.

- **Reconfiguration of UNRWA operations.** Enhanced policymaking and planning authority could be placed in the hands of Palestinian administrators in coordination with appropriate Palestinian councils and local groups in order to reorient service projects, upgrade their quality and plan for their integration into the Palestinian self-rule system. Preliminary steps could be taken toward determining the role that UNRWA would play during the interim period. A process could be set in motion to prepare camp residents for local elections early in the interim period.

Israeli-Palestinian Interaction

During the negotiations Palestinians and Israelis could seek ways to establish and deepen positive elements of their interaction.[26] This could serve to reduce Israeli fears about the potential consequences of relinquishing the OT and also demonstrate to Palestinians that there are Israelis who seek an altered relationship. More substantively, contact would build and enhance relations that would be important to successful interaction during the interim period and afterwards. Such interaction could include:

- **Israeli-Palestinian meetings to promote negotiations.** The one meeting in the OT held shortly after the Madrid conference was only permitted to have 200 Palestinians and 200 Israelis and had to be held in a closed school auditorium.[27] Encouragement for further meetings and elimination of restrictions on size and location would foster a more intensive and inclusive dialogue.

- **Palestinian-Israeli research on issues of mutual concern**. Specific research areas are noted in the security and economics sections, which could include joint teams to study and act on water and resource needs, human rights issues, and analyze the implications of different political scenarios for the long-range economic development and interaction of Israel and the OT. In recent months several such projects have been initiated by Israeli university teams and groups from Palestinian educational and research centers.[28] Meetings among educators and school children could increase in number and expand in scope. Collaborative research on cultural issues could be fostered. Studies could also be done on areas appropriate for joint economic investment.

- **Public conferences on relevant issues**. The results of joint research should be publicized and discussed in open forums that would receive press attention and emphasize the possibility of moving the relationship from hostility to cooperation. A planned joint academic conference on water issues, scheduled for fall 1992, would exemplify that approach.[29] Moreover, joint public discussions could be held on specific components of a peaceful Israeli-Palestinian relationship.

- **Israeli efforts to persuade the government to cease building settlements**. From the Palestinian perspective no step would be a stronger indicator of Israel's interest in reaching a mutually agreed solution. Israeli political and civic groups could intensify their efforts to end the expansion of settlements, through a wide range of public efforts. For example Peace Now has launched a major "settlements watch" charting government funds expended and housing starts initiated. Following the recent seizure of Arab homes in the Silwan district of Jerusalem a strong outcry from the Israeli public brought forth demonstrations — one led by Mayor Teddy Kollek — and established a permanent vigil at the site of other nearby Arab homes. There is continuing criticism from within Israel of the legal authority and political wisdom of land and home seizure and settlement building.

The Role of the PLO

The PLO, while not directly involved in the negotiations, would support the negotiations through continued political efforts and technical studies. The leadership would work to restore contact and credibility with key Arab states, deepen relations with the European Community, Japan and China, and bolster relations with Eastern Europe and the states of the former Soviet Union. Efforts to open channels of communication with the United States, in private if not in public, would be essential.

Technical support for the negotiating process is vital, with the Palestinians working in close coordination with Jordan on the range of legal, administrative, security and financial issues that would be critical to the interim period. Jordanian television and radio could be encouraged to broadcast programs, easily received in the West Bank, discussing political, social and economic issues central to the negotiations and to self-rule. Such broadcasts would reach people who do not have access to newspapers and would be responsive to oral and visual presentations.

Consideration could be given to the best means to represent the OT in the Palestine National Council (PNC), which serves as the Palestinian parliament in exile. Normally, a third of the PNC members would come from the OT, but their participation has been blocked by the Israeli government. Moreover, the PLO might change the method of representation in the PNC. Delegates might be elected directly by the four million Palestinians living in the diaspora, instead of the current system that sets quotas for particular political and mass groups, and allows the leadership to select non-affiliated members in the PNC. That change would help enhance the legitimacy and authority of the PNC at the grassroots level. UN monitors could help the PLO conduct the elections in sensitive countries in the region. If, at a later stage, OT residents could participate in the PNC, open elections for delegates would ensure their representativeness and public support. Elections would also provide a means for the Islamist movement, which currently has no parliamentary seats, to be represented proportionately in the PNC.

External Actors

External actors, particularly the United States and the European Community, would provide Palestinians with critical technical assistance and political encouragement in this bargaining process. Indeed, the ability of Palestinians to make meaningful progress toward real self-reliance, even in the context of limited self-rule, will depend on the degree to which their negotiations and their attempts at institution - building receive support from abroad. Without such support, the prospect that self-rule can be part of a genuine transition toward a satisfactory resolution of the Israeli-Palestinian conflict will diminish significantly.

In addition to meaningful political and technical support for the peace process, external actors could increase their involvement in economic projects (see Section III). Two aspects of their effort would be particularly important structurally and politically:

- They could encourage the strengthening of both local-level and OT-wide institutions that articulate and aggregate the interests of the Palestinian community with a view to encouraging coordinated planning and contributing to Palestinian self-reliance. The foreign donors would have to move sensitively among the indigenous political factions in order to avoid being perceived as favoring certain groups.

- They should insist that their own dealings with Palestinian organizations be carried out directly, unmediated by Israeli authorities. This would also directly support Israel's limited goal of allowing the Palestinians to handle their socio-economic affairs, and as such should be possible to carry out.

The Interim Period

Israel and the Palestinians will negotiate the explicit terms of any transition agreement. The examination that follows is offered as an exploration of the type of procedures and structures that the parties themselves will have to decide upon. Examples and potential suggestions are used to illustrate that concrete means are available to solve the specific problems of running a society on a day-to-day basis as it moves from occupation to some form of independence. This report assumes that well-organized means of self-government will serve not only the Palestinians in building the basis of a viable social order but also the Israelis by reducing the hostilities that existed during occupation and creating the forms of stability and order in Palestinian society that enhance Israel's own sense of security.

In order to have an effective interim self-governing authority (ISGA) in the OT during the transitional period, the basic design and underlying principles of institutional structures must be crafted during the negotiations. Their legitimacy might be enhanced through two sets of balloting: (1) a referendum to endorse the outcome of the negotiations and (2) elections to select the members of the governing body and ensure their accountability to the Palestinian public.

Principles Underlying Self-Rule

In the process of establishing the ISGA, basic principles need to be addressed.[30] The operationalization of those principles might, in some cases, take place over time:

- **The source of authority:** The negotiated agreement, on whose basis the ISGA would be established, would probably serve as the source of authority for the ISGA. In practice, effective power and decision-making would flow from the ISGA, not from a residual Israeli military presence. That de facto authority would expand and deepen during the course of the interim period as the indigenous institutions are solidified and assume control over a widening range of functions.

- **The ISGA's powers:** An effective ISGA would need the power not only to manage social and economic services but also to formulate public policy, to levy taxes and regulate financial matters, control police and security functions at the local and regional levels, and exercise at least joint control over land, water and other natural resources (see economics section for details).

- **Personal and territorial self-rule:** The territorial and personal aspects of self-rule are inextricably intertwined. Policy-making, planning, and economic stability necessitate the ISGA's having functional authority over public land and the guaranteed continuity of private land holdings. Territorial boundaries would also be delineated in establishing rules for maintaining internal security and the relationship between Israeli settlers and the Palestinian population. Thus, in operationalizing the ISGA, it is functionally inappropriate to separate the people from the land.

- **Participation by Palestinian inhabitants of East Jerusalem in the ISGA:** This may be one of the touchiest issues of the interim period considering the current wide difference between Israelis and Palestinians on the best way to resolve the status of Jerusalem. Some form of participation and representation of Jerusalemites in the ISGA would be essential to the stability and legitimacy of the ISGA, given the central importance of Jerusalemites to civic and economic life in the OT. For a Palestinian self-governing authority to have legitimacy among its people, Jerusalemites would have to participate in region-wide elections and be eligible to be part of the ISGA.

During the interim period, two simultaneous processes will take place. One will remove the current barriers to civic life, notably the restrictions on freedom of speech and assembly imposed by the military government and civil administration. The other will be the creation of structures that will have the potential to grow into state institutions. As Harvey Sicherman notes, such institutions "do not guarantee a state" but are "necessary building blocks" and make Israeli annexation more difficult.[31] A balance will be sought between the Palestinians' need to gain genuine authority over their lives as rapidly as possible and the current Israeli insistence that the transition not be automatic and irreversible. Thus, the establishment of interim institutions and transfer of authority will necessarily be a phased process, carefully calibrated to meet Palestinian and Israeli mutual needs.

Elections

Two sets of elections could be held, the first to ratify the negotiated agreement and the second to elect the ISGA. The elections would be preceded by a new census in the OT, undertaken by a joint team of Israelis and Palestinians with assistance from experienced UN personnel. The census would provide the basis for the electoral roll.[32]

A ratification process will be important for validating the negotiations and authorizing the formation of the ISGA. Otherwise, the legal basis and moral authority of the ISGA could be questioned by the public. A role in the ratification process should be sought for Palestinians abroad as well as in the OT in order to assure diaspora support for this interim phase. International agencies could be called upon for their help in this latter process.

Elections for the ISGA would be held soon after the negotiated accord is ratified. The central elections commission would be staffed by Palestinians, selected by the Palestinian negotiating team. Israeli civilian personnel and UN officials would monitor the process to ensure that the voting rolls tally with the census and that balloting remains free and secret. The basis for voting would be universal with voting age probably reduced from the current age of 21 (for municipal elections) to 18. Peaceful assembly and freedom of expression would be maintained during the election campaign, possibly with the presence of UN or other international representatives.

The preferred process would be the election of a 100-200 member ISGA, with individuals standing for election in each district or sub-district.[33] The ISGA would elect a chair and an executive body, responsible for overseeing the process of transferring functional authority from the Israeli military and civil administrations to the Palestinian departments. Each member of the executive body would head a department. The executive body would also have the authority, with the concurrence of the ISGA, to establish special commissions to deal with selected problems, as needed. For example, the ISGA would require a commission to revise the legal system as well as a civil service commission to supervise the transfer of functions and to review the conditions of employment of civil servants.

In the event that the negotiated accord does not provide for an elected assembly, a smaller executive council could be elected. Such an ISGA should have no less than 20-25 members in order to ensure its ability to maintain contact with all elements in the population and to enable it to operate the administrative departments effectively. That approach, however, would be less satisfactory than establishing a larger elected forum, since it would tend to reinforce traditional bases of authority and to overcentralize power in the hands of a small number of people.

Elections for municipal and village councils should be held within the first year of self-rule, assuming that they were not held at the end of the negotiating period. Elections should also be held in refugee camps, which would create municipal or village councils, depending on their size. District level administration would need to be revived, preferably with its officials elected by residents of the district; a special commission would draw up regulations to specify the legal and administrative relationship between the districts and the ISGA. The local and middle level tiers would help to enhance the accountability of the executive bodies to the community. Such accountability is vital to their legitimacy and effectiveness. Residents of East Jerusalem would be eligible to vote for the ISGA and to serve in the administrative bodies of the ISGA.[34] Any Jerusalem residents who would want to stand for election would have to maintain a second residency in a district of the West Bank or Gaza Strip.

The ISGA would also need to establish a system for legalizing and registering political parties. Persons would participate in the initial elections as individuals, but later elections could permit campaigns by political parties. A special commission would need to establish the procedures and criteria for approving the by-laws of political parties.

Development of Administrative Structures

During the first year of the interim period, responsibility for the existing administrative departments would be transferred to the ISGA and additional departments might be established. (See Figure 3 on pp.44-45.) The ISGA would appoint the heads of each department, who could be current or former employees or qualified persons previously holding non-governmental positions. The skeletal framework for administration is thus already present, even though staff and funds have been depleted. Comprehensive training programs will be required as well as an infusion of funds to upgrade equipment and buildings. In certain instances, such as the police and tax collection departments, employees who resigned during the *intifada* might be reinstated as well as new employees recruited.

The ISGA would need to have policymaking and financial authority over all the departments. That would include the ability to set and revise policy and programs in each department, control the budget, set and collect taxes and fees, and prepare medium and long range plans for programs and personnel. The ISGA would also have the power to hire, promote, fire and set standards for personnel in each department. The policies and programs in each department would be coordinated through the ISGA and the planning department. External defense and foreign policy would be excluded from the scope of the ISGA, but the ISGA would coordinate with Israel on internal security (see pp. 85-89). Joint Palestinian-Israeli bodies might be formed to handle and resolve issues related to electricity, water, and land during the interim period (see economics section, pp. 127-131).

Management training would be a vital component of institutionalizing an effective ISGA administrative system. Training in information systems, time management, personnel, and accounting would be valuable for departmental staff, for district officers, and for officials in municipal and rural councils. Professionalizing and up-grading the administration should be a priority early in the functioning of the ISGA. Women and people from disadvantaged communities should be particularly targeted in recruiting and training staff at all levels, to ensure that they are not excluded from operational and decisionmaking roles in the ISGA. Such efforts

Figure 3
Table of Administrative Departments*

Agriculture

Operate agricultural extension and research services; handle import and export regulation for produce; establish marketing centers to facilitate exports; provide and monitor veterinary services.

Communication and Transport

License and register vehicles; regulate the regional bus service; regulate and operate telephone, telefax and postal services.

Education

Operate public schools, including hiring, firing, and promoting faculty, regulating the curricula, standards, and extracurricular activities; register private schools and ensure educational standards; register universities, community colleges, teacher and technical training institutes, etc. and ensure educational standards; establish a system for comprehensive examinations (*tawjihi*).

Energy

Provide electricity to all towns, villages and refugee camps; ensure availability of fuel and other sources of energy.

Finance

Prepare budget of ISGA; collect direct and indirect taxes; disburse all public expenditures for other departments; solicit financial aid (grants, loans) from abroad for ISGA operations; handle any external government debt.

Health

Operate public hospitals, clinics, public health programs; register private health programs and ensure standards; plan long-term health programs, including preventive medicine, rehabilitation.

Housing

Prepare and implement public housing plans; license and regulate private construction outside of municipal boundaries.

Industry, Commerce and Cooperatives

Encourage private investment by individuals and cooperatives; establish regulations for and license industries, businesses, and cooperatives; license and regulate commercial banks and financial institutions; coordinate with Chambers of Commerce; regulate the tourist industry, maintaining standards for tour guides, restaurants, and hotels; coordinate with municipalities to establish industrial parks.

Information and Culture

Operate public radio and television stations; provide information on the performance of the ISGA; license newspapers and magazines; supervise cultural affairs, including archaeological excavations, and national museums arts programs.

Internal

Maintain internal security and supervise the police; issue IDs, register births, marriages, deaths, etc.; regulate municipalities, village councils, refugee camps; control use of public lands; run the public parks, national forests and nature reserves; plan and license construction outside municipal boundaries.

Justice

Control and regulate the magistrates courts, courts of first instance and the appeals court; revise laws to conform to the interim legal situation.

Labor

Regulate labor matters; establish labor codes and standards; coordinate with Education the development of vocational training.

Planning

Prepare regional development plans, in coordination with relevant departments; assist municipalities and local councils with planning; raise funds, in coordination with Finance; implement projects in coordination with relevant departments.

Public Works

Maintain roads, bridges, public buildings, etc.; construct new roads, bridges, and public buildings, including schools, hospitals, housing, in coordination with the relevant departments and local governments.

Religious Affairs

Coordinate with Muslim religious institutions, including courts, endowments (*awqaf*), schools, and holy places; coordinate with the Christian communities concerning courts, charities, schools, and holy places; guarantee freedom of access to all holy places; monitor conditions and status of religious pilgrims and help arrange for Muslims to travel on the *hajj* to Mecca.

Social Affairs

Assist the needy, elderly and handicapped; establish regulations for and license charitable societies, clubs, youth groups, etc.; coordinate with Education and Health in providing special education programs.

Water

Regulate domestic, agricultural and industrial water use; issue permits for drilling wells; provide technical assistance to construct reservoirs, dams and water networks.

---

* Most departments exist in skeletal form, covering only a fraction of these functions. Some have only Israeli staff; some differ between the West Bank and Gaza Strip. Departments for energy, housing, information and culture, and planning would be virtually entirely new. Basic data for the table was provided by Ibrahim Matar.

would help instill an emphasis on the importance of merit and technical skills in public life.

Interface with Existing Institutions

The ISGA would develop mechanisms for relating to existing structures in the OT such as the coordinating councils, UNRWA, and voluntary organizations. Its relationship with the PLO and other external Palestinian groups would also need to be addressed. In particular:

Coordinating Councils: We note three possible options: 1) Some councils might form the nucleus for the senior policy making bodies in the new and revived departments. The Council for Higher Education, for example, could assume responsibility for education and merge with the existing department; 2) Members of the councils might join the departments or special commissions but the councils might dissolve. In the agricultural, housing and industrial sectors, for example, the councils' functions would become redundant; and, 3) Some councils might continue as independent bodies, representing the interests of their constituencies vis-a-vis the ISGA and working directly with local Palestinian NGOs. The health and women's councils and committees are likely examples of that approach.

UNRWA: The ISGA would benefit from the experience of UNRWA in establishing procedures for its own civil service, but UNRWA's own structure would be gradually altered. Appropriate local level functions could be turned over to the elected councils in the refugee camps. The health and educational programs could be merged with the ISGA administration by the end of the interim period. The ISGA will need time to develop the capacity to manage those functions; suddenly assuming responsibility for UNRWA services could overwhelm it. UNRWA employees would not be automatically hired by the ISGA, but would have to meet the civil service criteria established by the ISGA.

Palestinian NGOs: The ISGA would institute rules for interacting with Palestinian voluntary agencies and charitable societies in a manner that would permit them maximum freedom and flexibility in their operations while ensuring the upholding of basic standards in, for example, health clinics or childcare centers. Voluntary associations should be encouraged to continue their dynamic efforts to mobilize at the grassroots level and to provide services to disadvantaged groups. They can also experiment with new approaches in ways that a government bureaucracy cannot afford to do. NGOs should be permitted to continue to receive donations and grants from abroad.

Relations with the PLO and other diaspora Palestinian organizations: The ISGA would need to regularize lines of communication with Palestinian institutions in the diaspora. Freedom to contact the PLO would be essential so that the Palestinians in the OT do not remain isolated from their compatriots outside and so that diaspora Palestinians will support actively the process of institutionalizing self-rule. Relations between the ISGA and the PLO could be further institutionalized if Palestinians from the OT were elected to the PNC, as mentioned in relation to the negotiating phase. If direct elections were not possible, the members of the larger ISGA forum and/or municipalities and village councils could be designated as representatives to the PNC. Such a development would also bring fresh faces and ideas into the ranks of the PNC. Discussions with the Israeli government would be essential to work out the form of interaction and representation, especially in the early stages of the interim period. Informal coordination would continue with PLO departments such as health, education, welfare, and planning and the PLO would retain primary responsibility for Palestinians in the diaspora.

Educational System

Possible policies and programs of the ISGA in the fields of security and economics are outlined in those respective sections. Two examples of departments concerned with services — education and health — will be examined here. They are critically important arenas for the Palestinians and ones in which the relations among institutions are particularly complex.

The ISGA would assume policymaking and administrative authority over the department of education and the public school systems in the OT. The Council for Higher Education, whose mandate (since 1990) covers private primary and secondary schools as well as community colleges and universities, could become the policymaking body for the department of education. The Council maintains close contact with Jordanian and Palestinian educational offices in Amman; therefore the transition could be relatively smooth. The educational officials would face multiple demands in the effort to improve the school system, including the need to:

47

- Establish unified curricula, teachers' salaries and working conditions for the West Bank and the Gaza Strip.
- Restructure teachers' salaries and benefits.
- Establish teacher-training workshops and in-service programs.
- Provide management training programs for school administrators.
- Review and revise the curriculum in all areas in order to bring it up to contemporary international standards and to encourage innovative pedagogical approaches.
- Revise the *tawjihi* (comprehensive) exam at the end of secondary school in order to unify the West Bank and Gaza exams and to create an indigenous exam system.
- Provide audiovisual and laboratory equipment and increase the relevant staff.
- Restore school libraries and librarians.
- Rehabilitate school buildings.
- Register, establish standards and guidelines for private schools.
- Foster parent-teacher associations in public and private schools.
- Coordinate and expand special education programs for physically and mentally disadvantaged persons.

Those will be daunting tasks. For that reason, the merger of UNRWA schools with the public school system might be delayed until the end of the interim period. Private schools will remain a small but important part of the educational system.

Changes may also take place in the community college and university systems, which are currently primarily private institutions. Some suggest that the universities merge into two large public universities, one in Gaza and the other in the West Bank, in order to reduce duplication in programs. Others feel that a system of locally based universities meets the needs of the community, even if it entails some overlap in courses. The unique personality and background of each university, coupled with the distances between towns and inadequate dormitory facilities, would tend to promote their continuation as separate, largely-private educational institutions. Educators agree that the current coordination should be enhanced and expensive programs should not be duplicated in each university. Additional changes needed include:

- Expansion of community college and university level education in the Gaza Strip, where the quantity and quality are seriously inadequate.

- Additional advanced programs at agreed-upon universities in legal studies, medicine, agriculture, and physical education.
- Expansion of the hotel management program at Bethlehem University to meet anticipated demand.
- A change in the policy toward community college graduates, so that qualified graduates could transfer to four-year programs, instead of finding that route an academic dead-end.
- Enhancement of the newly established al-Quds Open University system.[35]

Health Services

Responsibility for government health services would be quickly taken over by the ISGA. Unlike education, no coordinating council is positioned to provide effective policymaking authority and guidance. The Planning and Research Center (PRC) is trying to develop a national plan for medicine, but lacks the experience and authority of the Council for Higher Education. A plan would need to be developed based on local priorities, ensuring that health care is widely available in rural as well as urban areas, and emphasizing preventive and environmental approaches.[36]

The ISGA would have to rely on current and former staff from the health department and would have to undertake extensive training in managing health services. A comprehensive assessment of the quantity and quality of health care in hospitals and clinics would be required, with measures instituted to upgrade staff, bring in needed equipment, and rehabilitate hospitals. The lack of a medical school poses particular problems, since doctors have widely varying qualifications, depending on the country and institution in which they studied. Moreover, nursing schools are still minimal in relation to the need and no local programs exist for training middle-level technical staff or even ambulance drivers.

The clinics and primary health care programs run by Palestinian NGOs would continue to operate autonomously. Common standards would need to be established in order to ensure that they provide adequate care and do not duplicate each others' services in the same community. Internationally-funded hospitals, located particularly in Jerusalem, Bethlehem, and Gaza, would continue to provide vital services. UNRWA would maintain its clinics in refugee camps, the small hospital in Bureij camp (Gaza) and the currently-planned hospital in Khan Yunis, but UNRWA services would be integrated into the national system by the end of the interim period.

Contact with Israelis

Palestinian contact with Israelis would be extended and deepened during the interim period in order to help establish better human relations and to prepare for the transformations likely in the long term.[37] A significant expansion in public information efforts inside Israel would help to foster more constructive attitudes about Palestinians and Arabs. Attitudes which demonize Arabs need to be modified through new strategies for utilizing schools, the mass media, and direct exposure of Israelis to everyday Palestinian life. Comparable attempts to reduce stereotypes about Jews and Zionists would be made by Palestinians, including programs in the school system to bring together teachers and pupils in joint summer workcamps.

Israeli and Palestinian scholars could undertake collaborative research dealing with social, cultural and political issues common to Israel and the Arab world (economic cooperation is detailed in Section III). They might write for each other's publications, exchange university lecturers, support each other's professional organizations, and work on common curricula. The goal would be to increase mutual understanding and to clarify the benefits that both peoples would gain from peace.

A non-governmental group of Israelis could make a concrete contribution by developing contingency plans for relocating those Israeli settlers who do not wish to live under Palestinian authority at the end of the interim period. The group could encourage settlers to participate in the planning discussions, which could address among other issues compensation and assistance in resettlement. It could also address the rights, duties and protections envisioned for Israelis who prefer to remain in the OT and live under Palestinian authority. Efforts to develop such a plan would not only reassure Palestinians but would also enhance the debate within Israel on their realistic options. Further, a seriously drafted Israeli plan to deal with the issue of re-settlement could remove some of the ambivalence over territorial compromise that exists in the minds of many Israelis. They could feel less threatened by the compromises that would be necessary in the negotiations.

The Roles of External Actors

Foreign governments would provide crucial political support for not only the diplomatic process but also the institutionalization of the ISGA. They could emphasize the importance of international monitoring of elections. They could also seek to ensure that the ISGA has policymaking and legislative powers, including the right to levy taxes, control its budget, and license economic and social services. The governments could establish direct relationships with the ISGA, both on political matters and in the provision of financial investment and assistance.

Short-term financial and technical support for the administrative apparatus will be needed as the ISGA seeks to develop its operations. The brief description of the likely needs in the health and education spheres indicates the substantial requirements. Foreign assistance would be particularly timely in management and technical training to help guarantee the efficiency and effectiveness of the programs. Similar programs constructed at the local level would assist municipal and village councils as they gain greater authority.

The Long Term Status

Resolution of the Israeli-Palestinian conflict requires an end to occupation and mutual recognition between Israel and a post-occupation Palestinian sovereign authority (PSA), which would either form an independent state or confederation with Jordan. The framework of the current negotiations calls for opening negotiations on a final status agreement in the third year of the transition period. That structural transformation would transmute the current zero-sum struggle into a positive-sum relationship. All three peoples — Israeli, Palestinian and Jordanian — could achieve their core value of national self-determination, albeit on limited territory and with restrictions on its full operationalization by the Palestinians. The security of all three would be enhanced by a well negotiated agreement. Such a transformation would also contribute to ameliorating region-wide tensions and help to enable Israel to establish meaningful diplomatic relations and normalization of interactions with its Arab neighbors.

Although negotiations on the final status are not part of the current round and are scheduled only in the third year of an interim self-governing arrangement, many of the steps taken in establishing the ISGA would be sharply influenced by the probable final status agreement. The institutional and administrative forms would vary widely if continued Israeli sovereignty or control were envisaged as compared to some form of independence. This report is predicated on the latter outcome. The discussion of the forms of authority below is suggestive not prescriptive.

Scope of Palestinian Authority

A successful conclusion to the peace process would mean that Palestinian institutions established during the interim phase would become fully independent and fully functioning. Their precise nature would vary, depending on whether Palestinians gained an independent state or joined with Jordan. The PSA would have authority across the spectrum of political and public policy issues, including foreign affairs, defense (within negotiated limits) and the use of natural resources. Its status would be guaranteed by the United Nations, in which it would have full membership. The international legal analyst Gidon Gottlieb argues that even if the PSA were linked to Jordan:[38]

> It could be given international standing separate from and in addition to that enjoyed by Jordan in the international community, without in any way affecting or modifying Jordan's own status. On a formal juridical plane no obstacle exists to giving an entity that forms a part of another sovereign state full membership in the community of nations.

The PSA would have authority to determine the status, rights and obligations of Israelis who choose to live in the Palestinian territory. Similarly, the PSA would have authority to establish and implement national policy concerning relations with Palestinians in other countries, including the conditions under which they might return to the PSA-controlled territory.

The PLO would in all likelihood merge with the PSA institutions, in the territory and abroad. PLO diplomatic missions would be transformed into embassies of the PSA. Residual PLO offices, absorbed into those embassies, would assist Palestinians who remain in the diaspora. Some, though not all, Palestinian staff would work in administrative or technical positions in the PSA. The PLO charter of 1964 would be explicitly superceded by documents establishing the PSA and therefore would be annulled *de jure* as well as in practice.

Return of Palestinians

The issue of the right of Palestinians to return has stirred deep fears among Israelis and caused deep yearning among Palestinian refugees. Israelis fear that Palestinians would insist on returning to their homes inside Israel from which they fled in 1948. According to the Palestinian professor Rashid Khalidi, however, the Palestinian concept of return has evolved substantially over time.[39] Palestinians, he argues, view the right as inalienable but understand that once they accept Israel's right to exist they can only implement the right within the part of the land that comprises the Palestinian state. Palestinians whose families originated in what is now Israel would, in practice, receive compensation but would not return to their former homes.

The PSA would have the right to decide how many refugees would be settled in the territory it controls and at what rate, in keeping with the availability of resources to absorb them. Priority might be given to those Palestinians who face the greatest difficulty in the diaspora: the Palestinian community in Lebanon, especially those in refugee camps, who cannot be fully absorbed by that fragile state, and the Palestinians who fled Kuwait in the wake of the Gulf crisis and can neither return nor be successfully absorbed in Jordan. Those who have citizenship and residency in Jordan are not likely to return unless they originate from the West Bank or Gaza. In fact, some Palestinians might move to Jordan during the interim or final periods, particularly if a Palestinian-Jordanian confederation were formed.

Palestinians who continue to live in the diaspora would have their legal status regularized. Some would gain permanent residency in their host state while holding a Palestinian passport; others might be invited to become citizens in the host country, retaining the right to visit the Palestinian homeland. Arabs should be encouraged, within the context of a regional settlement, to extend such residency and citizenship rights. Gottlieb notes: "A national passport would express for every holder the emotional and symbolic bond that unites the Palestinian people."[40]

Because the continuation of a Palestinian refugee problem constitutes a potential threat to Israeli security — as a base for recruiting armed groups — compensating refugees and resettling them in a way that grants them citizenship either in Palestine or in host Arab states would be important for Israeli security. Moreover, Palestinians would welcome the resolution of the problem of property confiscated from Jews who fled Arab countries after 1948 as part of a regional effort to mitigate the human tragedies caused by that conflict.

Jerusalem

The complex issue of Jerusalem will come to the fore in the final stage. The city has unique dimensions that require special provisions. Both Israelis and Palestinians tend to rule out redividing the city, with physical barriers separating the two parts. They also reject internationalization, although some Arabs would welcome international protection for the holy places in the Old City. Although current Israeli law asserts an exclusive right to control the city, as the country's eternal capital, the international community has never accepted that interpretation. (See Figure 4.)

Other options exist that would recognize the legitimacy of both the Israeli and the Palestinian presence and rights in the city. The Israeli political scientist Naomi Chazan has outlined four options:[41]

Single sovereignty: Jerusalem would be the capital of one state but administrative functions would be shared.

Split sovereignty: Jerusalem would be physically united and the capital of both states; administrative functions would be shared or divided.

Joint sovereignty: Israelis and Palestinians would govern the city together, with all functional institutions integrated on an equitable basis.

Shared sovereignty: The territorial bounds of Jerusalem would be extended to encompass an equal number of Israelis and Palestinians. Sovereignty would be divided between the two peoples, with joint supervision of the holy places and a shared administrative umbrella in which Israelis and Palestinians would have equal representation; the chairmanship would rotate.

At present, Israelis tend to prefer the "single sovereignty" option with Israeli maintaining its sovereignty over the city. Palestinians prefer "split sovereignty." However, creative solutions would be possible in the final stage, once the mutual tensions and suspicions are reduced. Already, leading Israelis and Palestinians are meeting to discuss ways in which dual sovereignty could be operationalized.[42] Nearly fifteen years ago, the Palestinian scholar Walid Khalidi suggested that the principles for resolving the issue of Jerusalem should be "non-exclusivity, co-equality, non-dominance, co-sharing, non-coercion, palpable justice..., the non-dictation of spiritual hierarchies."[43] He sought to allay Israelis' fears by main-

Figure 4
Jerusalem

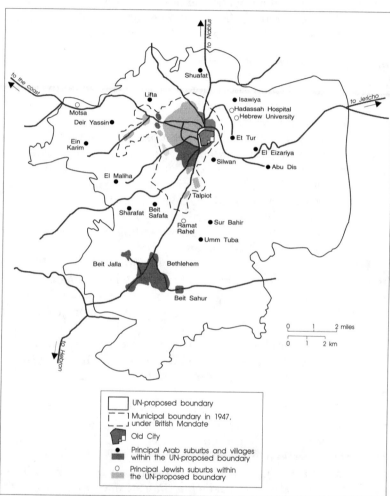

On 29 November 1947, as part of its resolution on Palestine (Resolution 181(II)A), the General Assembly of the United Nations adopted the proposal that "The City of Jerusalem shall be established as a *corpus separatum* under a special international regime and shall be administered by the United Nations."

Source: *The West Bank and the Gaza Strip* (Palestinian Academic Society for the Study of International Affairs, East Jerusalem, 1990).

taining that "an irreversible right of access to the Wailing Wall would be an integral part of the settlement, while a special regime for the Jewish-owned properties adjacent to the Wailing Wall could be created." The pursuit of imaginative solutions will be an important aspect of creating a viable accord on Jerusalem.

Settlements

The issue of Israeli settlements in the OT is equally thorny. Gottlieb suggests that the only way that Israelis could justify on nationalist and ideological grounds the removal of settlements would be if they distinguish between the "state" of Israel and the "land" of Israel: the "land" would encompass the West Bank and Gaza Strip, but the limits of state authority would be narrower geographically.[44] Similarly, Palestinians would distinguish between the land and the territory: the PSA's authority would cover the Palestinian state or confederation, which would be only part of the historic Palestinian land. These understandings would be firmly set as part of the negotiated agreement.

Phrased differently, both peoples would distinguish between their ethnicity and their nationality. Jews who choose to remain under the jurisdiction of the PSA would be loyal citizens of that state, while maintaining their support for Israeli nationalism, just as Jews are full citizens of other states while upholding Zionist ideals. Palestinian citizens of Israel would maintain a similar dual identity: their allegiance would be to the state of Israel while they would support the existence of a Palestinian state (or confederation) under the PSA.

Given an interim period in which Israelis would adjust to their gradual disengagement from the OT and provisions would have been made for the reintegration of settlers into Israel, the prospect of evacuating settlements would appear less traumatic than it does today. Nonetheless, that issue will be difficult to resolve without leaving tension between Israelis and Palestinians and without the risk that feelings of irredentism would remain among Israelis. Similarly, some Palestinians would retain irredentist desires. Both Israeli and Palestinian government and political leadership would be needed to provide a new vision for the citizens of both societies and take steps to ease the perceived losses.

Endnotes to Chapter I

1. Liberal use is made of draft materials written by Ruth Klinov, Everett Mendelsohn, Shibley Telhami, and Mark Tessler in writing these sections. Other sources are cited in endnotes.

2. Yitzhak Shamir statement to *Le Monde*, 23 April 1991, quoted in Kenneth W. Stein and Samuel W. Lewis, *Making Peace Among Arabs and Israelis* (Washington, D.C.: United States Institute of Peace, 1991), p. 24.

3. *Jerusalem Post* (International Edition), 13 June 1992, p. 6 and 20 June 1992, p. 4.

4. Quotations in this and the following paragraph are from Meir Shamgar, "Legal Concepts and Problems of the Israeli Military Government — The Initial Stage," in Meir Shamgar, ed. *Military Government in the Territories Administered by Israel, 1967-1980: The Legal Aspects*, Vol. 1 (Jerusalem: Hebrew University Press, 1982), pp. 13, 22-28, 53. Shamgar was Military Advocate General, then Attorney General and then a justice on the Israeli High Court.

5. Civil administration did not mean either civilian administration or Palestinian administration. The first civil administrator in Gaza was an Israeli army officer. The first civil administrator in the West Bank was an Israeli professor, who had served as political advisor to the Military Governor. See Palestinian Academic Society for the Study of International Affairs (PASSIA), *The West Bank and Gaza Strip*, Jerusalem, 1990, pp. 63-64.

6. An Israeli staff officer was in charge of each department. During 1967-68, six other Israelis served in the postal and phone services, seven Israelis in health, and eight in social welfare, all in supervisory positions. Palestinian teachers on the West Bank went on strike in fall 1967, and won some concessions from the military government concerning textbooks, curriculum, and the authority of Palestinian education officials. (A.M. Lesch. *Israel's Occupation of the West Bank: The First Two Years*, RAND Research Monograph, 1970, pp. 5-9, 16.)

   According to Aryeh Shalev, *The Autonomy* (Tel Aviv University, 1980, p. 157), as of December 1978, there were 11,165 Palestinian employees in the West Bank (including 6,668 teachers, 1,370 health workers, 382 in agriculture, and 290 policemen). There were no senior Palestinian employees in statistics, personnel, taxes, customs, religious affairs, archeology, abandoned and state property, commerce and industry, employment, interior, telecommunications, electricity and treasury; and no Palestinians worked in the customs offices or as prison guards. However, there were senior Palestinian employees in health, agriculture, water, justice, welfare, public works, surveying, post office, and transport. In transport, all the directors were Israelis and only they had the authority to issue licenses. In the Gaza Strip, the 4,829 Palestinian employees included 1,848 teachers, 1,362 in health, 120 in agriculture, and 429 police. Each office had an Israeli officer-in-charge plus a Palestinian appointee-in-charge, some of the latter at director-general rank, who handled routine matters.

Sara Roy, *The Gaza Strip Survey* (Jerusalem: The West Bank Data Base Project, 1986, p. 13) indicates that 5,426 Palestinians worked in the government sector in the Gaza Strip in 1986, including 2,468 in education. Eighty-eight Israelis worked in the Gaza civil administration.

Shamgar, p. 444, gives slightly different figures for the West Bank: (a) education: 14 Israelis and 913 Palestinians in May 1968, but 12 Israelis and 8,316 Palestinians in December 1980; (b) health: 9 Israelis and 800 Palestinians in May 1968, but 15 Israelis and 1,403 Palestinians in December 1980; and (c) welfare: 10 Israelis and 104 Palestinians in May 1968, but 9 Israelis and 165 Palestinians in December 1980. (His figures for the Gaza Strip include Northern Sinai and thus are not usable here.)

7. Munir Fasheh, "Education under Occupation," in Naseer H. Aruri, ed., *Occupation* (Belmont: AAUG Press, 1989), pp. 513-535, and *Educational Network*, No. 7 (February 1992), published by the Friends Schools, Ramallah. Shamgar, pp. 445-6, says the number of government schools decreased on the West Bank from 884 in 1967-68 to 790 in 1979-80 even though the number of pupils increased from 107,332 to 199,437. His figures for the number of pupils per teacher include government, UNRWA and private schools: the overall ratio worsened from 26 in 1967-68 to 29 in 1979-80. Comparing Shamgar's figures for the number of pupils in only government schools and the number of "classes" in those schools (assuming that each class has one teacher), the ratio is 32.6 in 1967-8 and 34.6 in 1979-80. Ghassan Abdallah, director of the Center of Applied Research in Education (CARE), told the author on 7 January 1992 that government school teachers are paid 15 percent of Israeli teachers' salaries, lack clothing or transport allowances, and must teach as many as sixty children, often with broken blackboards, outdated textbooks, and no visual aids. CARE, the Tamer Institute for Community Education and other groups of educators in private and UNRWA schools try to hold seminars on, for example, educational leadership, innovative instructional methods, and Arabic spelling mistakes, but the civil administration bans public school teachers from attending those training sessions. CARE prepared a pamphlet for teachers to update the history texts (which still refer to Libya as an impoverished monarchy), but Abdallah worried that the Israeli officials would ban teachers from using it in government schools.

8. Union of Palestinian Medical Relief Committees, "Health and Health Services under Occupation," in Aruri, ed., pp. 417, 421; PASSIA, pp. 54-56.

In 1991 Israel allowed UNRWA to begin constructing a 232-bed hospital in Khan Yunis, with initial funding from the European Community.

9. Moshe Drori, "Local Government in Judea and Samaria," in Shamgar, pp. 244, 253.

10. Peace Now figures note that from 1967-1990, 20,000 houses were built in settlements. Peace Now maintains that 98,500 Israelis live in the West Bank, not the "official" 120-130,000. *Jerusalem Post* (International Edition), 1 February 1992, p. 2.

11. In the Gaza Strip, municipalities are also responsible for drinking water supply for residents. PASSIA lists and discusses the municipalities, pp. 51-54, 63-64; Drori in Shamgar, pp. 242, 245-254, 275; Lesch, *Israel's Occupation*, p. 12; Lesch, "Prelude to the Uprising in the Gaza Strip," *Journal of Palestine Studies* (20:1, 1990), p. 5.

12. Lance Matteson, Middle East representative for ANERA, in a paper submitted to USAID, quoted in "Middle East Trip Report" of Peter Gubser, ANERA president, November 1991, p. 12.

13. Drori in Shamgar, pp. 243, 272-274; PASSIA, pp. 51-52.

14. The four elections in 1972-73 were in Jenin, Jericho, Nablus, and Qalqilya (the latter being a new chamber, separated from Tulkarm); no elections were held then in Bethlehem, Hebron, Ramallah, and Tulkarm (Drori in Shamgar, pp. 255-8, 266-272), or in the Gaza Strip or East Jerusalem. In 1991, elections were held in Gaza, Hebron, Jericho and East Jerusalem, and in 1992 in Ramallah and Nablus: see economics section for more information. See also PASSIA, p. 62. The federation is mentioned in Salim Tamari, "Revolt of the Petite Bourgeoisie: Urban Merchants and the Palestinian Uprising," *The Palestinians: New Directions*, ed. Michael C. Hudson (Washington, D.C.: Center for Contemporary Arab Studies, Georgetown University, 1990), p. 27.

15. For lengthy discussions of the harassment of unions and their internal problems, see Lisa Taraki, "Mass Organizations in the West Bank," in Aruri, pp. 446-451; Joost Hiltermann, "Mass Mobilization and the Uprising: The Labor Movement," in Hudson, pp. 44-62; and Hiltermann, *Behind the Intifada: Labor and Women's Movements in the Occupied Territories* (Princeton: Princeton University Press, 1991). On unions in Gaza, see also Lesch, "Prelude to the Uprising...," p. 12; PASSIA, p. 62.

16. There were also ten private community colleges, which accommodated 4,333 students, 19 percent of post-secondary students, in 1987 (an eleventh college was opened later). UNRWA and government training centers accommodate another 14 percent, totalling 3,192. Bir Zeit University had become a two-year college in 1962, but expanded to four years in 1972. Several post-secondary institutions upgraded to universities, including Freres College, which became Bethlehem University in 1973, al-Najah National University in Nablus in 1977, the Islamic University in Gaza in 1978, and Hebron University in 1980. Al-Quds University was formed in 1981 to serve as an umbrella for four colleges:

the College of Paramedical Sciences (el-Bireh), the College of Science and Technology (Abu Dis), Women's College of Art (Jerusalem), and al-Daw'a College of Islamic Studies (Beit Hanina). PASSIA, pp. 33-38; Fasheh, p. 525 and Naseer Aruri, "Universities under Occupation," pp. 491-510, in Aruri.

17. PASSIA, pp. 18, 24, 26; Fasheh in Aruri, p. 513.

18. Matteson in Gubser, p. 12.

19. For overviews, see Taraki, pp. 434-446, Lesch, "Prelude to the Uprising," and A.M. Lesch, *Political Perceptions of the Palestinians on the West Bank and the Gaza Strip* (Washington, D.C.: The Middle East Institute, 1980).

20. The four women's committees are (1) Palestinian Union of Women's Work Committees, originally founded in Ramallah as the Women's Work Committee; (2) Union of Palestinian Working Women's Committees; (3) Palestinian Women's Committees, and (4) Women's Committees for Social Work. Taraki in Aruri, pp. 457-462, describes their efforts, which range across basic services (day care centers, summer camps for children, primary health care), education (first aid, literacy, child care, sewing), productive work (toys, pickles, biscuits etc. made at home and in workshops), and mobilization (visits to prisoners' families, demonstrations, and increasing awareness of women's and national issues). See also Hiltermann, *Behind the Intifada*, and Islah Abdul Jawwad, "The Evolution of the Political Role of the Palestinian Women's Movement in the Uprising," in Hudson, pp. 63-76.

21. The four committees are (1) the Union of Palestinian Medical Relief Committees, established in 1979, which had 370 voluntary doctors and a network of mobile and permanent clinics by the late 1980s; (2) the Popular Committees for Health Services, set up in 1981; (3) the Union of Health Care Committees, linked to the Women's Action Committee; and (4) Health Services Committee, a registered non-profit association. (Glenn Robinson, "The Role of the Professional Middle Class in the Mobilization of Palestinian Society: The Medical and Agricultural Committees," forthcoming article in *The International Journal of Middle East Studies*.) Robinson also notes (relevant to the next sentence in the text) that the peripheralization of notable leadership was made possible by structural changes: 1) increased wage labor, 2) land confiscation with partial depeasantization, and 3) increased university education, especially for the lower and lower middle class, all of which expanded the politically relevant strata of the population.

22. See A.M. Lesch, "Contrasting Reactions to the Gulf Crisis: Egypt, Syria, Jordan, and the Palestinians," *The Middle East Journal* (45:1, winter 1991), especially pp. 46-48.

23. Plan entitled "Ideas for Peaceful Coexistence during the Interim Period," presented at the Israeli-Palestinian negotiations on February 20-21, as quoted in *The New York Times*, 27 February 1992, pp. 1, 8; and

full text in *al-Fajr*, 9 March 1992, p. 16, along with the letter from the head of the Israeli delegation to the head of the Palestinian delegation.

24. *The New York Times*, 27 February 1992, p. 8; and full text, entitled "Expanded Outline: Palestinian Interim Self-Government Arrangements: Concepts, Preliminary Measures and Elections Modalities," mimeo, 3 March 1992, 12 pp.

25. *Al-Fajr*, 25 November 1991, p. 6, reported that Palestinians who wanted to restore Palestinian control over the Gaza municipality argued that the city desperately needed the repair of basic services and resumption of social and development projects for sewage, water, and electricity. Dr. Zakaria Agha, a member of the Palestinian negotiating team from Gaza, maintained that the timing was inappropriate, since those issues would be discussed in the peace talks.

26. Some of the ideas come from Aloush Hareven's "Educational Policies" background memorandum for AAAS, and some from an Israeli-Palestinian meeting at the Stanford University Center on Conflict and Negotiations in July 1991, entitled "Framework for a Public Peace Process," quoted in *al-Fajr*, 23 September 1991, pp. 8-9.

27. *Jerusalem Post*, International Edition, 14 December 1991, p. 11 reported on the formation of political committees. When Peace Now joined Palestinians in a rally on November 13 called "People Speak Peace" in the auditorium of the Friends School in Ramallah, the military government specified that no more than 200 Israelis and 200 Palestinians could participate, according to Peace Now News (newsletter of Americans for Peace Now, 7:2, Winter 1991), p. 1.

28. The Israel/Palestine Center for Research and Information, for example, had convened fifteen roundtable meetings of Palestinian and Israeli economists and businessmen by February 1992 and fourteen meetings of Palestinian and Israeli water specialists; hosted an ongoing forum on Jerusalem and, in April 1992, launched a forum to promote dialogue among Israeli and Palestinian educators on issues of cross cultural curricula. According to *ICPRI News* (no. 4, April 1992, p. 5) the latter would investigate such issues as how each side would wish to see its own culture, history and traditions taught in the other side's schools and how both sides could create educational frameworks to bridge the gaps caused by hatred, fear and misunderstanding.

29. An academic conference is planned on water issues for October 1992, linking the Applied Research Institute of Jerusalem (a Palestinian development agency) and the Truman Research Institute for the Advancement of Peace at the Hebrew University. That conference grew out of the forum hosted by IPCRI, mentioned above.

30. For an interesting discussion of those issues, see Danny Rubinstein in *Ha'aretz*, 24 October 1991, as translated in *al-Fajr*, 4 November 1991, p. 10. Shalev, writing in 1979, noted (pp. 79-80) that the Israeli stance in the autonomy talks was that the IDF and military government would

remain the authority, which would give it the right to intervene and decide concerning legislation, land, water etc. However, the then ministers of defense and agriculture argued that the agreement itself would be the source of authority, not Israel. Shalev believed that the latter was the logical solution, in which case, if the Israeli government wanted to limit autonomy or reserve rights to itself, it would have to define those rights and include them explicitly in the autonomy agreement.

31. Harvey Sicherman, *Palestinian Self-Government (Autonomy): Its Past and Its Future* (Policy Paper no. 27, The Washington Institute for Near East Policy, 1991), p. 77.

32. If it proves impossible to conduct a census, current IDs could serve as the basis for participating in the referendum and ISGA election. But a census would need to be conducted during the interim period, which would serve as the basis for issuing ISGA IDs and conducting future elections.

33. Some of the ideas in this section are adapted from Gershon Baskin's draft proposal, "The Interim Peace Phase - Palestinian Self Rule," 20 November 1991; Baskin is co-director of the Israel/Palestine Center for Research and Information (IPCRI), Jerusalem. He suggests that the SGA be composed of 100 representatives, with 68 elected from sub-districts and 32 elected on the district level (4 representatives for each of the current 8 districts). That formula, however, does not represent each inhabitant equally: the heavily populated Gaza Strip and the currently sparsely populated Jordan Valley each comprise one district, with the same representation. A formula based on population — such as one representative per 50,000 inhabitants — would be more equitable.

34. Baskin proposes to have Jerusalem residents elect a separate council which will not be part of the ISGA but will serve as a self-rule authority until the final status of Jerusalem is determined by the parties. The Palestinian SGA in Jerusalem would work in conjunction with the Israeli municipality in Jerusalem and would retain responsibility for functional authority in Palestinian neighborhoods of Jerusalem, including internal planning.

35. Initiated in May 1991, the Open University enrolled 2,500 students in 1991-92, operating out of its headquarters in Jerusalem and six regional offices. *Masterplanning the State of Palestine* (Center for Engineering and Planning, Ramallah, 1992), p. 126.

36. A preliminary report on the national health plan was presented in *al-Fajr*, 8 June 1992, p. 3.

37. Suggestions are based in part on the fora organized by IPCRI, noted earlier, and the background memoranda for AAAS by Tessler, Hareven, and "Human Rights" by Edy Kaufman and Mubarak Awad; also the Palestinian-Israeli statement, "Framework," in *al-Fajr*, 23 September 91, and comments to the AAAS study group by PLO spokesperson Bassam Abu Sharif, Tunis, 25 July 1991.

38. Gidon Gottlieb, "Israel and the Palestinians," *Foreign Affairs* (68:4, fall 1989), p. 116. He cites the cases of Byelorussia (Belarus) and Ukraine, which had full membership in the UN while they were part of the USSR. Gottlieb's own preference is for a tripartite confederation, involving Israel, Palestine and Jordan.

39. He argues that Palestinian negotiators would seek the repatriation to Israel of a limited number of refugees, particularly in the context of family reunion, but recognize that only a token number would be allowed into Israel. Rashid I. Khalidi, "Observations on the Palestinian Right of Return," *Emerging Issues*, Occasional Paper no. 6 (Cambridge, MA: American Academy of Arts and Sciences, October 1990). Note also Moughrabi et al, "Palestinians on the Peace Process," *Journal of Palestine Studies* (XXI:1, autumn 1991), p. 49, and Laurie A. Brand, "Palestinians in the Diaspora," background memorandum for the American Academy.

40. Gottlieb, "Israel and the Palestinians," p. 123.

41. Naomi Chazan, "Negotiating the Non-Negotiable: Jerusalem in the Framework of an Israeli-Palestinian Settlement," *Emerging Issues*, Occasional Paper no. 7 (Cambridge, MA: American Academy of Arts and Sciences, March 1991), pp. 17-18, 23-24. Other proposals include that of Mark Heller in *A Palestinian State* (Harvard University Press, 1983), pp. 121-126. He suggests that, given Jerusalem's emotional centrality to both peoples, no conventional political formula is possible. He frames Israel's objectives as (1) the physical and administrative unity of Jerusalem, (2) free and secure access to all parts of the city and control of Jewish religious sites, (3) maintaining strategic control, and (4) legitimizing its status as Israel's capital. Heller argues that those four objectives can be realized by making Jerusalem the capital of both Israel and Palestine (with each having its executive organs, legislative body, judiciary and foreign legations in the city), establishing a joint municipality (with a Jewish mayor and Palestinian deputy mayor and considerable devolution of powers to neighborhoods), setting up a joint police force, and having each state handle access to the city at specified points of entry. Israeli troops would not be positioned inside the city but would be placed at the eastern edge to control access to the coast. The current borders of the city would be modified slightly so that Qalandiya airport (at the north end) would be outside the city limits and under the control of the Palestinian state.

42. *IPCRI Newsletter*, October 1991, no. 3, pp. 6-7. IPRCI's Jerusalem roundtable prepared a document as a model for Jerusalem, based on the concept of an open city with no physical division but two municipal councils, each with governing authority over specific areas. Standing or ad hoc committees would coordinate issues of joint concern, particularly involving the Holy Places, Old City and infrastructure. Mark A. Heller and Sari Nusseibeh in *No Trumpets, No Drums: A Two-State Settlement*

of the Israeli-Palestinian Conflict (New York: Hill and Wang, 1991) suggest a complicated formula by which Jerusalem would be the capital of both Israel and Palestine; religious communities would control religious and personal status issues (along the lines of the Ottoman *millet* system); separate municipal councils would handle each ethnic neighborhood; and an overarching municipality, elected by all the residents, would be responsible for zoning, infrastructure, sanitation and security matters (pp. 121-123).

43. Walid Khalidi, "Thinking the Unthinkable: A Sovereign Palestinian State," *Foreign Affairs* (56:4, July 1978), p. 706.
44. Gottlieb, pp.117-8. Heller and Nusseibeh argue that there is "no room for extraterritoriality or extended sovereignty for Israeli settlements within a Palestinian state." (p. 103) Although settlers would not be evacuated forcibly, they would be provided with financial incentives to leave. Those who remain could become Palestinian citizens or live as Israeli citizens who are permanent residents of Palestine (pp. 105-6). The Palestinian Interior Ministry would establish regulations for the residency of foreigners.

II

External and Internal Security

If a period of interim self-government is to be built and succeed it is in the area of security that Israelis and Palestinians must develop the strongest mutual understanding and confidence. Ironically the least serious thought and preparation has been given to the issue of security.* The very word security has significantly different meanings for Israelis and Palestinians and evokes very different responses in each community. While both share a core concern for the safety and survival of their own community their perceptions of what needs to be done at present to achieve security are largely asymmetrical. Israelis focus on the external threats from the potentially hostile military forces of Arab regional powers; military security in an unstable region largely governs their understanding and planning. Their direct engagement in five significant wars since 1948 has set the tone and priorities of almost all Israeli security discussions. A second Israeli concern is that of "terrorism," attacks across their borders by small, armed groups aimed at creating fear and public insecurity.

For Palestinians, on the other hand, their status under military occupation serves as the commanding problem confronting the security and well-being of their community. Explicit military considerations lie largely outside their current perceptions while they concentrate on achieving freedom from occupation and the ability to maintain community order. Israelis are concerned with the long-term aspects of a military and strategic nature; Palestinians are primarily concerned with the more immediate and proximate dimensions of communal security.

---

* Security issues are dealt with briefly in this text and are to be treated more fully in a report being prepared by another study group being convened by the American Academy of Arts and Sciences.

When it looks at the OT Israel frames its security needs primarily in the context of the strategic military threat posed by regional states rather than in the context of its direct relationship with the Palestinians. While it is clear to Israelis that their military power is disproportionate to that of the Palestinians, Israel perceives itself as disadvantaged strategically in the wider context of the Middle East. Therefore many Israelis look at the potential security advantages of controlling the territories of the Golan Heights and West Bank, recognizing that the inhabitants pose little military threat. The nature of a negotiated Arab-Israeli security regime would therefore influence in significant ways the form of a Palestinian-Israeli security arrangement in the OT. Improvement in Israel's external security environment would affect the willingness and ability of the Israeli government to reduce its military presence in the OT and to allow the ISGA to assume control over internal security functions. Thus, a significant aspect of achieving a negotiated agreement between Israelis and Palestinians will involve creating mechanisms to underwrite the internal and external security of both peoples, given asymmetries in power and position. Throughout the negotiating process, both sides must maintain the principle that security is a *mutual* need. Adjustments must be made for asymmetries in power and position in order to reinforce the legitimacy and stability of a comprehensive regional security system.

A stable security regime encompasses political, economic, and social dimensions. Peace agreements will provide vital insurance for a long-term security regime, since national rights will accrue to the Palestinian community, trade and labor flows will be normalized for mutual benefit, and diplomatic relations will be established between Israel and the neighboring Arab states. A recent Israeli-Palestinian gathering suggested: "The peace agreement by itself will reduce motivation for war and hostility in the region. Political stability in the region, resulting from a comprehensive peace settlement, will reinforce security in the region. Economic prosperity and interdependence will ensure the common interest in maintaining a lasting peace."[1]

The Status Quo

Israeli External Security

Neither Israelis nor Palestinians are secure at present. Israel's external security is threatened by the hostility of key regional states. Israel has diplomatic ties and mutual security arrangements with Egypt alone among the Arab states. Gottlieb terms Israel a "diminutive territory with no strategic depth,"[2] vulnerable strategically, especially to a surprise attack from the East. Israeli strategic doctrine relies on launching preemptive strikes and moving the fighting rapidly into enemy territory in order to preserve intact the vulnerable coastal zone in which most Israelis live and where industrial development is concentrated. In this security vision the occupation of the West Bank and Golan Heights provides Israel with territorial depth in case of a land attack as well as a small amount of additional time to react to an air strike. The OT provide locales where troops can be mobilized and an attack deflected from Israel's vulnerable heartland. Early warning stations and troops along the Jordan River and on the Golan Heights guard against conventional attacks and prevent armed guerrillas from infiltrating. Israel's hold on the OT ensures that Jerusalem, Tel Aviv, and key airports are out of range of small arms and mortar attack.

Israel maintains buffer zones on all sides: the zone seized and held in south Lebanon, the Syrian Golan Heights, the West Bank facing Jordan, and Egypt's negotiated, largely demilitarized Sinai peninsula. The Israeli navy patrols the Mediterranean Sea and seals off the Gaza Strip. This comprehensive security system has been imposed unilaterally by Israel with the exception of the bilateral accords on Sinai and the Golan. Buffer zones guard against threats to Israel's survival. Indeed, the initial Arab successes in the war of October 1973 appeared to confirm the military value of territorial buffers: Israel was able to absorb the first strike by Egypt and Syria across the Suez Canal and the Golan Heights without serious risk to its pre-1967 territory. Similarly, the buffer zone in south Lebanon enables the Israeli armed forces to prevent most attacks by armed Lebanese or Palestinian groups crossing the border or mounting artillery barrages against northern Israel.

The buffer zones have been supplemented by tacitly agreed "red lines" beyond which Arab forces must not move without anticipating an Israeli military reaction. In Lebanon, Syrian troops are warned against moving south of the red line at the Litani River. In Jordan, the red line would be crossed if Iraqi troops entered Jordanian territory. Israel, however, did cross an implicit red line when its forces seized sections of the Beirut-Damascus highway in 1982. A related concept of deterrence lies in the implied threat to bomb Arab cities if Israeli population centers are hit. That red line apparently deterred Syria and Egypt in 1973. The Israeli air force, however, did bomb Beirut in 1981 and 1982. Israel's possession of nuclear weapons, while not formally acknowledged, poses a potential strong deterrent to Arab states should they use weapons of mass destruction against Israel or should they threaten Israel's existence by conventional means.

The Gulf war, however, necessitated reappraisals of Israel's strategy. The confidence in the assertion of strategic superiority, coupled with the maintenance of buffer zones and red lines, was shaken even by the limited threat posed by Iraq's Scud missiles. The senior Israeli military analyst Ze'ev Schiff comments that the political requirements of the allied war effort meant that Israel had to absorb the Iraqi strikes without launching retaliatory counterstrikes, even though the Scuds hit the country's heartland; this emphasized the vulnerability of civilian lives, and reinforced Israelis' sense of being besieged.[3] Israel had to rely on Patriot antimissile batteries rather than its own forces. It further turned out that Israel lacked an adequate civil defense infrastructure. The buffer zones or strategic depth to the East did not make the Israeli heartland invulnerable in the face of surface-to-surface missiles launched by a distant country. Military and intelligence surveillance proved inadequate and Israel's strategic vulnerability was underlined. Iraq could potentially harm the relatively small territory of Israel with ground-to-ground missiles located 600 kilometers away in western Iraq more effectively than Israel could damage Baghdad (1000 km distant) or harm the extensive Iraqi territories by using comparable weapons. Nonetheless, Iraq did not cross the most dangerous red line and use chemical weapons. Schiff stresses that the crisis could lead Israel to expand anti-missile defenses, enhance sophisticated military intelligence devices, particularly via satellites, and increase such civil defense measures as the construction of bomb shelters. The crisis thereby widened the scope of Israel's security perimeter well beyond the occupied territories, the buffer zones and red lines established in the past.

Israeli Internal Security

Israelis are also concerned by threats to their population emanating from the OT. The military and police must protect Israelis from violent acts by Palestinian civilians, which include throwing molotov cocktails, planting bombs, and shooting or knifing Israelis, both in the OT and inside Israel. For example, from mid-January to early February 1992, the press recorded a half dozen attacks in

Israel, East Jerusalem and the West Bank. They included the death of an Israeli at a building site in Rishon LeTzion, his skull cracked by a blunt instrument, and the wounding of seven Israelis and the Palestinian bus driver by gunshots fired at a bus driving on a main road of the West Bank to Shiloh settlement. That marked the fifth attack on settlers since negotiations began in late October. In those attacks, four settlers died. In the Old City of East Jerusalem, two religious Jews were pummeled by youths as they walked to the Western Wall; a Palestinian woman was arrested as she tried to set fire to a police car near the Western Wall; and police arrested two teenage Palestinian girls, apparently on the grounds that they carried knives with which they might attack Jewish worshippers.[4] Such incidents enhance the sense of insecurity pervasive among not only Israeli settlers but also among civilians living in Jerusalem and inside the pre-1967 territory. The vulnerability even of military forces inside Israel was underscored when three soldiers sleeping in an encampment were stabbed to death in February 1992, apparently by Palestinian citizens of Israel who lived in a nearby village.

Diminishing such violence is vital to the Israeli public, but there is no consensus as to how to effect that change. Some call for strengthened direct control and argue that Palestinian violence makes imperative Israel's permanent control over the OT. Ze'ev Binyamin Begin, of the Knesset's subcommittee on national security policy, maintains that Israeli settlements and military control are essential in order to prevent Arab "terror groups" from dominating the West Bank and threatening the security of West Jerusalem and Tel Aviv.[5] Begin's argument assumes that Palestinians are implacably opposed to Israel's existence as a Jewish state on Palestinian land and can only be contained by force.

Other Israelis argue that the occupation itself provokes the Palestinians' reaction and conclude that the burden of policing Palestinians against their will has become increasingly unbearable.[6] The policing function drains the armed forces both financially and in personnel. Scarce military resources must also be diverted to protect the Israeli settlers, whose very presence provokes a militant reaction among Palestinians. Occupation corrodes and undermines the military, whose role administering civilian affairs has weakened their preparedness for their primary mission of securing the country from external threats. Moreover, rather than reducing the potential for external violence, occupation makes Israel a continuing target from the outside by keeping alive the grievances that could lead to continued instability and a potential all-out Arab-Israeli war. Labour Party leader and new Prime Minister Yitzhak Rabin notes that occupation in itself fuels Palestinians' hatred and "territorial compromise can bring us a life of peaceful coexistence with them as with our other neighbors."[7] Finally, given the need to reduce the Israeli budget, the military must establish priorities: should priority be given to sophisticated weapons and defense systems or to policing the Palestinians in the OT? The strategy of external military deterrence and forcible control internally has become increasingly problematic in its effectiveness and increasingly costly to carry out. Schiff concludes that the risks incurred by ruling the OT may be "greater than the benefits they accord."[8]

Palestinian Insecurity in the OT

For Palestinians their overriding sense of threat to communal security and well-being comes from the Israeli military occupation and its consequences. Palestinians feel insecure in their personal lives and as a community. Their insecurity takes significantly different forms from Israel's insecurity. Palestinians living in the OT have limited security of person or property. They are vulnerable to a variety Israeli actions against which they have little legal or political recourse.

Their catalogue of daily challenges to what they consider their security concerns is long. Palestinians may be arrested without specific charges brought against them; they can be deported into permanent exile without serious legal safeguards. (East Jerusalemites, however, are considered residents of Israel and therefore are rarely deported.) Palestinians can be detained in poor prison conditions for substantial periods without charge or trial. Detainees in Ketziot prison (Ansar III) in the Negev desert, for example, live in crowded, open tents with inadequate food and medical care and infrequent access to their lawyers and families. Those who stand trial before military courts cannot gain credible legal protection; the judges, who owe their loyalty to the same military government that arrested the person, routinely ignore evidence of torture or forced confessions and impose heavy sentences and fines for even minor infractions.

Palestinians face severe restrictions in their daily lives, in addition to the political and economic constraints that are noted elsewhere: extended curfews, restrictions on movement, forcible tax collection, seizure of property, and closure of institutions. Public demonstrations are forcibly suppressed; during one week in November 1991, shortly after bilateral negotiations began, soldiers trying to block demonstrations wounded twenty-five Palestinians and injured an additional seven persons with teargas. Soldiers also forced their way into seven schools in the OT, where they beat, gassed and arrested students.[9]

Palestinians face the rigor of lengthy curfews, during which they are forbidden to leave their houses or even sit in their gardens. Children have been shot when they wandered into the alley to play. Obtaining food is only possible if the curfew is lifted briefly and if bakeries and grocery stores are permitted to function. Residents often cannot take ill persons to the hospital during a curfew, since they risk being shot if they walk or drive on the road.

Residents of the OT are subject to restrictions in their movement: special permits are required to move within the territories as well as between the OT and Israel. Access to and through Jerusalem has been blocked, preventing Palestinians from traveling between the north and south sectors of the West Bank, denying access to places of worship as well as to the economic, social and cultural centers in East Jerusalem, and disrupting family and social contact. Moreover, exit to and entrance from Jordan across the Damiya and Allenby bridges are strictly regulated for political as well as security reasons. Bridge permits are often denied to residents of an entire village or town as punishment for political activities.

Income taxes are sometimes collected by force. Armed security personnel break into a house, shop or office to seize documents, furniture, machinery or electronic appliances in lieu of cash. A family can be left with virtually no furniture after a tax raid and a factory can lose all its equipment and inventory.

Palestinians also lack security of property. Their land can be confiscated, their orchards uprooted and their houses demolished, all without effective legal redress. In the same week in November 1991 cited above, 75 acres were confiscated on the West Bank; 600 acres were seized the week before. Settlers buried 50 olive trees under loads of dirt and the army uprooted 500 olive trees. The army also demolished 23 houses claiming that they were built without permits.

The frequent closure of schools and universities restricts access to education and thereby diminishes the prospects for the younger generation. Bir Zeit University has suffered the most severe restrictions: it has been closed on the basis of a continuous series of three-month military orders for four years and only in the spring of

1992 was allowed to reopen partially. Even elementary schools were closed for extended periods during the intifada.

These profound violations of personal and communal security, persisting during the twenty-five years of occupation, have affected Palestinians deeply. They do not control the institutions vital to them and lack the means to seek redress against violations of their security.

The Palestinian police and court system are controlled by the Israeli military government. Most Palestinian policemen fled from the West Bank to Jordan in 1967, leading the military government to recruit and train replacements, who remained unarmed.[10] Virtually the entire police force resigned during the intifada, leaving a vacuum in law enforcement.

Three separate court systems exist in the OT: the system in the Israeli settlements, the military courts, and local Palestinian courts. One court system serves Israeli settlements on the basis of Israeli civil, criminal and religious law. Since 1984, the Israeli officer in charge of the judiciary must consent before a Palestinian can register a complaint against an Israeli citizen; in practice, even common crimes by settlers against Palestinians are tried by Israeli courts, not the local Palestinian courts.

Second, military courts and tribunals handle not only security cases but also — at the discretion of the military commander — criminal cases and financial violations, in such areas as traffic, drug abuse, customs, bribery, licensing, and foreign currency. The Military Objections Committee handles appeals against land expropriation and income tax assessment. The military governor must approve any legal proceeding against Israeli government officials, members of the army, or their employees.[11]

Third, local courts which pre-date the occupation have been transformed by Israel.[12] Israel forbade appeal to the highest court, the Court of Cassation, located in Amman, and transferred that function to the West Bank Court of Appeals, which it moved from East Jerusalem to Ramallah. The lowest tiers — magistrates' courts and the two courts of first instance (district courts) in Hebron and Nablus — continue to function, with diminished responsibilities and reduced resources. The post of inspector of courts was abolished, with the responsibilities turned over to the president of the Appeals Court. Judges are appointed by the Israeli Ministry of Justice and, since October 1967, Israeli lawyers have been allowed to plead in Arab courts. Although virtually all Palestinian lawyers refused to practice in the years immediately following 1967, by now more than

200 Palestinian lawyers take cases to local or military courts. However, the Palestinian lawyers are not allowed to practice in East Jerusalem or Israel, since they cannot become members of the Israeli bar; thus, they cannot take cases on appeal to the Israeli High Court and must rely on Israeli (Jewish and Arab) lawyers. The military government has prevented the Palestinian lawyers from forming a professional association that could maintain standards, represent their interests and monitor developments. Thus, the Palestinians lack many of the means by which they can maintain the rule of law and enforce legal judgments.

The deterioration of normal legal functions has undermined efforts to curb violence by Palestinians against other Palestinians. Although the leadership of the intifada attempted to establish a process by which an alleged collaborator would be warned and tried in secret before facing execution, in practice individuals and groups have taken action on their own against Palestinians. Youth squads attack individuals accused of collaboration and Islamist-oriented groups pressure women to dress and behave in a manner that they view as appropriate and challenge other community activities deemed to be religiously unacceptable. Some Palestinians fear that such attacks degenerate into personal or clan vendettas; when a member of Fatah's Black Panthers stabbed to death in Tulkarm a teenager affiliated with Hamas, the prospect of inter-factional killings also emerged.[13] The lack of an effective local court system or indigenous police force limits the Palestinians' ability to control such actions and thus exacerbates the sense of insecurity pervasive in the community.

Palestinian Insecurity in the Diaspora

Another dimension of the sense of threat to the broader Palestinian community comes from problems faced by the nearly 4 million who live in the diaspora. Palestinians who reside in Arab countries live in politically and economically insecure conditions. The approximately 1.5 million Palestinians who live in Jordan have acquired citizenship, but unspoken restrictions still block access to sensitive military positions and surveillance is tight in refugee camps. In other countries, Palestinians are not granted citizenship and therefore have no passport for travel or means to secure protection. Palestinians long resident in Egypt (roughly 100,000), Lebanon (350,000) and Syria (300,000), for example, can travel only if they obtain a special document valid for the particular trip. Palestinians living in Egypt have to pay for schooling and hospital care and cannot own agricultural land or work in the public sector.

Palestinians in Lebanon also cannot attend public schools or hold government jobs; work permits in the private sector are difficult to obtain. The PLO therefore had established factories and clinics to help the Palestinian residents and, when the civil war broke out in 1975, tried to protect camp dwellers from Lebanese militia attacks. When the PLO forces had to evacuate Beirut in 1982, many refugees lost their protection against the militias and Israeli forces.

Palestinians who work in the Gulf states can only remain as long as they are employed; they are denied full ownership of shops or other property and must leave when they retire. Their individual professional success in the Gulf can be swiftly undermined by political crises. The Palestinians' insecure status was underlined when the Kuwait government engaged in collective punishment against the Palestinian community after the Gulf war. The government dismissed Palestinians *en masse* and banned their children from attending public schools. With their work and residence permits invalidated, most had to leave, carrying minimal possessions and only their severance pay with them to Jordan.[14] The PLO lacks the diplomatic stature and political clout to protect Palestinians living in the diaspora from such restrictions and deprivations; the organization's status is insecure and dependent on the goodwill of the host regimes.

The insecurity of the Palestinian situation in the diaspora is compounded by the current virtual impossibility of their returning to live in the OT. Those who were abroad in June 1967 can visit only on the basis of temporary permits from Israel. Strict criteria are enforced: a visitor must be a first-degree relative — parent, spouse, sibling or child — of a resident in the OT. Few receive permission to reside permanently in the OT. Even that limited permission is frequently denied, despite the hardship caused to families. After a series of forcible expulsions of wives and children in 1989-90, the Israeli high court ruled in June 1990 that those family members should not be expelled.[15] Nonetheless, persons who arrived in the OT since that ruling are still threatened with deportation.

Negotiating Phase

Given Israel's dual external and internal security concerns, negotiations must address both sets of issues and point toward a reduction in threat in both realms. For Palestinians in the OT, in contrast, priority in the short run would be placed on reducing internal insecurity by enforcing human rights standards in the OT and by reducing Israel's power over their daily lives.

For negotiations to bring substantive changes to the lives of Israelis and Palestinians, both parties will need to take steps to enhance security for themselves and each other. Such steps would create tangible benefits for their communities and would have a positive psychological impact, reducing the climate of fear. Each side would see risks inherent in the steps they would need to take, and therefore would need reassurances from the other party and from third party sources. The measures would occur in the context of the changes in the civil and economic arenas and would need to involve a sense of mutual benefit in order to be acceptable. Given the severe imbalance of power in the OT, the most obvious initial steps to build confidence would have to be disproportionately taken by Israel. Nonetheless, important reciprocal actions by the Palestinians would be necessary in order to indicate their intentions to establish a mutually secure future for both peoples. Moreover, the bilateral and multilateral negotiations with Arab governments could have the effect of buttressing the Israeli-Palestinian talks and provide a context in which Israel could significantly reduce restrictions on life in the OT.

Alleviating Israeli External Security Concerns

Bilateral Israeli-Palestinian negotiations are taking place in the context of comparable talks with Syria, Lebanon and Jordan. The latter open up the possibility of Israel's achieving strategic accords with its immediate neighbors. Multilateral negotiations that include the Gulf states also introduce the prospect of regional arms control accords, including establishing a zone free of weapons of mass destruction. Successful negotiations would make Israel less dependent on unilaterally imposed buffer zones and on its technological superiority. They would enmesh Arab governments in a regional system that would provide enhanced security for all the parties. Particular components of negotiations might include:

- **Syria:** Issues of sovereignty and demilitarized buffer zones in the Golan Heights, diplomatic recognition, and verifiable arms limitations comprise the essence of these negotiations; a phased accord along the lines of the Sinai agreement could restore Syrian sovereignty while retaining the zone as a demilitarized buffer to

Israel's north-east. A limited forces zone might also extend into Syria, east of the Heights.

- **Lebanon:** Key components of the negotiations involve establishing diplomatic relations in the context of restoring the Lebanese government's control over its southern territory and providing assurances of an end to armed guerrilla incursions into Israel; the establishment of mutually-agreed security structures in the south would be a vital aspect of such accords.

- **Jordan:** Negotiations concerning diplomatic recognition and security arrangements along the extended common border would alleviate tension and uncertainty on the critical eastern front. Israel is also interested in agreements that prevent Jordan from becoming a staging point for other Arab forces — notably Iraqi troops — to launch an attack against Israel.

- **Iraq:** UN-imposed measures to destroy Iraqi weapons and end its capacity to make chemical and nuclear weapons would significantly reduce the threat in the short term, but would need to be buttressed by a long-term regional arms accord.

- **Regional arms control:** Multilateral negotiations to regulate arms acquisition and limit weapons of mass destruction and long-range missiles would create the possibility of a long-term beneficial shift in Israel's security environment. In the short term these limitations may constrain the Israeli nuclear deterrent. In the longer term such limitations will constrain the potentiality of the development of an Arab nuclear capability as well.

Negotiations between Israel and its Arab neighbors on security issues would, if productive, positively influence Israel's approach to security in the OT. If Israel could anticipate reduced tension with its Arab neighbors in tandem with establishing Palestinian self-rule, then its requirements for maintaining a visible military presence in the OT to ensure external security would be reconfigured. Such regional accords would enhance the possibility of Israel's countenancing a substantial withdrawal of its armed forces and, instead, protecting Israeli territory through demilitarization of the OT and the maintenance of technical early warning systems.

In order to help conceptualize those negotiations, Arab and Israeli academic analysts could develop strategic plans that would detail the provisions essential to the transitional period and a stable security system. Off-the-record meetings among Israelis, Jordanians, Lebanese and Syrians would initially be confidential, but ultimately their findings would need to be made public for use by negotiators and as a means of reassuring the populations of all the parties. The plans might deal with regional issues as well as phased implementation, demilitarization and monitoring of accords related to the OT. Joint analyses would serve to reassure all parties that mutual security concerns could be addressed effectively and that each side is sensitive to the other's insecurity and fears. Moreover, they would help third parties comprehend and encourage sequenced, reciprocal moves that would build confidence and momentum to carry forward a transition.

Israeli Measures to Promote Security in the OT

During the process of negotiations, steps can be taken which would decrease the level of tension in the OT and thereby foster a climate more conducive to an accord. Israeli confidence building measures would serve to indicate the government's determination to achieve a stable political settlement based on concepts of mutual security.

A number of specific measures would facilitate the negotiating process itself and enable Palestinians to engage in open political debate concerning their future. Those include Israeli steps to:

• Accord limited diplomatic immunity to the Palestinian negotiators so that they need not fear arrest or harassment.

• Permit political meetings in halls without requiring prior security license.

• Cancel censorship of newspapers and other publications to permit free discussion of diplomatic, political and related issues.

• Lift restrictions on the movement of Palestinian residents among the West Bank, Gaza and East Jerusalem so that normal economic and social activities can resume.

• Allow educational and other civic institutions to function without restriction.

Another set of measures would reduce public insecurity and help create a climate conducive to an accord. For example, Israel could:

• Stop arresting residents without formal charges or conducting full court proceedings.

• Release administrative detainees, held without trial or public charge.

- Grant amnesty to prisoners such as children and sick persons, as goodwill gestures.[16]
- End deportations, including the expulsion of family members who lack residency documents.
- Minimize the use of military patrols within cities, villages and camps and stop their forced entry into homes.
- Assert control by the armed forces over the behavior of settlers, including prosecution of settlers for killing or injuring residents or damaging property.
- Refrain from using military forces for non-military actions, such as tax collection and confiscation of documents from homes and offices.
- Cease such collective punishments as sealing or demolishing houses and imposing curfews over the civilian population.

While one would not anticipate, during negotiations, moves to resolve the issue of the return of Palestinians from the diaspora, emergency measures could be taken on humanitarian grounds that would reduce tension and demonstrate tangible goodwill by allowing some return to the OT. The government could, for example, address the problem of Palestinians who fled Kuwait during the Iraqi occupation or were later compelled to leave by the Kuwaiti government. At least 300,000 fled to Jordan, of whom 30-40,000 have been allowed by Israel to return to their original homes in the OT. An additional 18-20,000 Palestinians who had lived in Kuwait came from the Gaza Strip on Egyptian laissez-passers. Those documents do not permit them to live in Egypt or travel to Jordan. Most lost their jobs in Kuwait, but remain trapped there and risk forcible deportation. A humanitarian gesture by Israel to allow those who want to be repatriated to Gaza to return there would have a positive impact, even if relatively few took up the offer.[17]

Application of the Fourth Geneva Convention

There is a continuing debate within Israel, and between Israel and the international community about the applicability of the Geneva Convention for the Protection of Civilian Persons in Time of War (August, 1949). Although Israel is a signatory to the Convention, successive governments claim that the West Bank and Gaza are not in fact occupied territories of another state and therefore the Convention does not apply. The governments have claimed that on a voluntary basis they are guided by some of the Convention's humanitarian provisions.

Civil rights advocates in Israel and international human rights organizations contend that actual enforcement of the convention would maintain human rights standards on a more secure basis than the independent measures taken by Israel. The UN Security Council continues to maintain that the convention applies to the OT, including Jerusalem.[18] For Palestinians, this is a crucial issue. Moreover, its application would enable Palestinians to frame their concerns in the context of enforcing internationally recognized basic rights. For example, the convention prohibits the deportation of residents from the OT, the transfer of Israeli civilians into the OT, collective punishment, and the expropriation or destruction of property when not justified by military necessity. In this context the proposed confidence-building measures could be rephrased as fundamental issues of human rights, including:[19]

• The right to education: open schools.
• The right to worship: access to holy places.
• The right to mobility and travel: end restrictions.
• The right to access to one's job: end curfews, travel restrictions and confiscatory fines and taxes.

The presence of international observers in the OT is urged by many human rights advocates; they would help to enhance the application of the convention and could go a long way to smooth relations between the Israeli authorities and Palestinian residents during the negotiations. UNRWA officials already play an informal but important role in monitoring human rights conditions not only in the refugee camps (which is their official venue) but also in nearby towns and villages. This *de facto* legitimization of the principle of an international presence could be institutionalized and expanded. Moreover, the International Committee for the Red Cross (ICRC) has a longstanding formal presence in the OT, quietly documenting human rights violations, seeking to ameliorate conditions in prisons and to improve detainees' access to lawyers, and assisting persons whose homes have been demolished. Such systems of international monitors could later help ensure the independence of elections for the interim self-governing authority (ISGA) and ease the transition in internal security arrangements during the interim period.

Even without the application of the Fourth Geneva Convention, international support could be directed to strengthening Palestinian and Israeli human rights organizations as a means of enhancing the defense of their people's rights. Moreover, during the negotiations, groups on both sides could undertake joint efforts to promote human rights and raise awareness in their communities concerning the importance of resolving core security concerns. Joint committees might be set up and joint teams might address critical human rights problems that could arise during the interim period and that could jeopardize Israeli-Palestinian security. Such efforts would also serve the longterm interest in creating conditions for democratization, by encouraging respect for the rule of law, fostering representative forces within Palestinian society, and preventing a deterioration in human rights standards in Israel.[20]

Palestinian Confidence-Building Measures

Palestinians would also need to take tangible steps during the period of negotiations. Such confidence-building measures would indicate to Israelis that Palestinians are ready to live beside them in peace once the occupation regime is ended and thus show that the security needs of both communities can be met. Those measures would also enhance security within the Palestinian community.

Palestinian leaders indicate that actions would occur spontaneously once Israel adopts the above-mentioned measures to reduce restrictions and open up political discourse. The senior advisor to the Palestinian delegation, Faisal Husayni, commented:[21]

> If the army will withdraw from cities and villages, it will reduce clashes by a significant percent. A release of prisoners would create a new situation. Instead of going to demonstrations, people would hold political meetings... The intifada is a reaction to Israeli actions. Violence engenders counter-violence. If the Israeli actions change, the intifada will assume another face and protests will become more non-violent. This will happen on its own, people will feel it; there is no need for an order.

Such changes, Husayni noted, would also alter the "atmosphere among the Israeli people: civilians, soldiers and even the leaders. Things that look impossible now may ultimately become acceptable to the Israeli side." Those spontaneous shifts, however, are explicitly conditioned on prior Israeli actions. The movement toward mutual confidence building would be enhanced if simultaneous, reciprocal steps could be taken; efforts toward this end should be explored and supported by unofficial groups in both communities.

Nonetheless, a crucial asymmetry exists between the Israeli and Palestinian leaders' ability to control violent actions by members of their communities. Palestinians lack courts and police that could enforce order; appeals by individual politicians to reduce violence and focus on non-violent modes of protest, while important, cannot be followed up by effective action. Individuals and political groups opposed to the negotiations or personally aggrieved continue to use violence to attain their ends. In contrast to the very limited forms of control by Palestinian leaders over instruments of police power, the Israeli government has police and military forces under its command. Those forces could enforce its will by limiting violence by Israeli settlers or political forces that seek to undermine the Israeli negotiations or provoke Palestinians into striking back violently.

Despite the asymmetry, visible efforts would be essential on the part of leaders and organized groups in the OT as well as the PLO leadership outside to take clear positions and make all possible efforts to counteract the use of violence during the period of negotiations. Those efforts, which in several cases would involve repeating and reinforcing already-stated guidelines, include:

- Condemnation of armed attacks by Palestinians against Israelis and other innocent bystanders.[22]
- Condemnation of widening the violence to include civilian targets inside Israel and emphasizing that protest should be confined to the OT.
- Condemnation of terrorism by reiterating the PNC resolution of November 1988 and implementing the PLO's commitment to discipline groups that attempt to attack Israel.
- Condemnation of violence by Palestinians against other Palestinians and enhancement of efforts to prevent personal vendettas and extrajudicial execution of putative collaborators and criminals.[23]

Efforts of this sort would be intended to alleviate Israelis' deepset existential fears and at the same time reduce intra-Palestinian insecurity. Their clear impact would not come until the establishment of the period of interim self-government with its intricate security arrangements. Only then could there be a tangible improvement in security. The ISGA would, by its institutions and actions, be able to prove its commitment to mutual security and stability. Until that point, both sides would remain wary of each other's confidence-building measures. Palestinians would fear that Israeli measures could be rescinded at will, and Israelis would fear that a lull in violence could be followed by a renewed upsurge.

A specific statement, made now by the Palestinian negotiators, that might begin to shift Israelis' perceptions, would be a unilateral declaration that the Palestinian entity and eventual state would be demilitarized and committed to peaceful relations with Israel. That declaration would indicate that Palestinians have no intention of threatening Israeli security and only seek their right to govern the OT.[24] Moreover, a declaration of demilitarization would address an important rationale used to argue for Israel's control over the territories thereby altering a critical element in the Israeli cost-benefit calculus. Withdrawal from the territories would begin to seem affordable in security terms and potentially a more viable option than the current Israeli control.

The Interim Period

Restructuring security arrangements on the ground will be an essential component of the interim period. New arrangements for external and internal security would be established by negotiations and tested in practice by Israelis and Palestinians. The changes would be made on a mutually-agreed, phased basis, which would give time to build confidence in the durability of the new security regimes. In addition any successful implementation of Israeli-Arab accords would further alleviate tension and enhance Israel's position regionally. Such steps while important as additional supports should not become a condition for Israeli-Palestinian agreements on a transition regime. Palestinian-Israeli accords would provide the basis for reducing Israeli control over the Palestinians and enhancing Palestinians' rights and secure existence, and would thoroughly restructure the now tense and unsatisfactory relations between these two communities.

Israeli Accords with Arab States

The feasibility of instituting a substantial Israeli military withdrawal from the OT and maintaining only limited forces on the Jordan River and at key points would be related primarily to the signing of peace treaties and establishment of security arrangements with Israel's Arab neighbors. The Israeli military analyst Ze'ev Schiff notes that, so long as Israel remains in a state of war with Syria and Jordan, the government would insist on stationing troops in the West Bank for protection against external threats. These troops do not, however, need to be involved in policing the local inhabitants or stationed in or near Palestinian population centers. (The Gaza Strip would be of less concern, given the peace accord with Egypt, the sizeable buffer zone across Sinai, and the effectiveness of the Israeli navy's patrols along the coast.)[25] The implementation of accords with key regional powers would bolster Israel's external security and substantially ease the process of Israeli military disengagement from the Palestinian OT. Agreements would be essential along the following lines:

- **Syria:** The Golan Heights would be demilitarized, on a phased timetable, in the context of a peace treaty and the establishment of bilateral diplomatic relations, including an enhanced international presence to ensure compliance by both sides. Israeli early-warning stations would remain on Mount Hermon (Jebel al-Shaykh) during the interim period and a limited forces zone east of the Heights would restrict the presence of Syrian troops west of Damascus. Syrian civilians would gradually return to their homes and provision would be made to relocate Israeli settlements.

- **Lebanon:** A bilateral peace treaty would provide for the Lebanese army to regain control over the border area in conjunction with international forces. Lebanese and Palestinian militias would be disbanded, the latter with a formal agreement with the PLO. An Israeli-Syrian accord would detail the provisions for mutual restraint on Lebanese territory.

- **The PLO:** Assurances from the PLO that it would endorse and uphold the interim security measures would be underlined by the agreement to disband its forces in Lebanon and by actions to discipline individuals and groups that attempt terror attacks on Israel, on Israelis abroad or on third parties.

- **Iraq:** The UN-imposed restraints on Iraqi weapons systems and remilitarization would need to be buttressed by negotiated accords with the Iraqi government. A direct Israel-Iraq agreement is highly unlikely, but their mutual security concerns could be alleviated in the medium-term by regional arms accords and by international commitments to limit Iraq's rearmament.

- **Regional arms control:** Multilateral agreements to limit specific categories of arms, notably weapons of mass destruction and related delivery systems, would be essential for starting to reduce the regional arms race. Measures for verification on the ground and by satellite would be integral to the accords.

Israeli-Palestinian-Jordanian Security Relations

During the interim period, the nature of Israel's military presence in the OT would be vitally affected by the negotiations with Jordan. The concern does not lie with Jordan's own intentions and military power but, as the Israeli strategist Dore Gold argues, with the possibility that a revived Iraq could move mechanized units across Jordan more rapidly than Israel could call-up its reserves.[26] In the context of a peace accord with Jordan, therefore, Israel would be able to consider a more rapid and substantial redeployment of forces in the West Bank than it would in the absence of such an agreement. Nonetheless, throughout the interim period, Israel would insist that its external security needs be met primarily through its own armed forces and it would remain wary of withdrawing significantly from militarily important installations in the West Bank. Its troops would regroup in mutually agreed locations in the OT and maintain the current system of electronic and aerial early warning stations. International monitors might play a role in reassuring each party about the other's compliance. Possible provisions include:

- Phased withdrawal, over the course of the five year interim period, of Israeli forces from the army camps and installations in the central areas of the OT. The rapidity of the withdrawal would depend on the nature of the accord with Jordan and on the phased establishment of a security regime by the ISGA.

- Redeployment of Israeli forces to specific sites in the Jordan Valley, for example the two bridge crossings and limited locations at the extreme north and south of the valley. The negotiations would determine the size of Israel's troop presence along with arrangements to use land between the IDF and the ISGA and private Palestinian owners. International monitors might be included in the deployment to reassure Jordan and the ISGA and to help monitor the security situation along the river.

- Control over security at the Allenby and Damiya bridges and at the Rafah crossing to Egypt would remain in Israeli hands, but international observers might monitor the procedures. Officials from the ISGA internal affairs department would check and register IDs and handle any customs payments on imports.

- Maintenance of limited Israeli forces to guard existing stations on the mountaintops in the West Bank for advanced warning against air attack, perhaps supplemented by international monitors. The

84

exact number, location and size of the Israeli presence would be determined in the negotiations, along with the leasing arrangements.

- Assurance of Israel's right to resupply stations on the mountains and in the valley, using designated roads and agreed-upon times and with adequate warning of troop movements.

- Specification that the mission of the Israeli forces on the Jordan River and at early warning stations would relate to external security, not internal policing.

- Maintenance of the right of the Israeli air force to overfly the airspace of the OT and the prohibition of other air forces from overflying the territories.

- Continuation of Israeli naval patrols off the coast of the Gaza Strip, with mutually agreed provisions for boarding vessels suspected of carrying armaments or armed persons to or from the territory.

- Establishment of an Israeli-Palestinian-Jordanian commission to address contested issues involving external security, border controls, etc.

A Jordanian-Israeli peace treaty would include provisions for mutual security along their border north and south of the West Bank. Joint patrols might be established along the border, with international monitors or tri-partite teams to ease compliance. Designated border crossings could be established in the Beisan (Beit Shean) area and at Eilat and Aqaba.

Internal Security in the OT

The Israeli strategist Aryeh Shalev argues that "the matter of internal security seems to be the hardest and most complicated one to solve, for if there is no security, there is no peace."[27] Nonetheless, he stresses, clear and practical arrangements are essential so that the lines of responsibility and control would not be blurred. Immediately after the interim agreement is signed, the Palestinian negotiators would declare an official end to all the violent aspects of the intifada and a halt to all violence against Israelis. The Israeli government would simultaneously pledge to halt acts of violence against Palestinians and to curb all violence by Israelis against Palestinians.

In order to provide authority to the ISGA and expect the ISGA to assume increasing responsibility for internal security, the negotiated agreement would serve as the legal basis for the emerging political system. The military administration would be phased out of existence and a process would be undertaken by which the ISGA would review and alter the military decrees promulgated since June 1967, restore authority to the civil courts, revive the local Palestinian police force, and establish procedures for maintaining internal security and operating prisons. The ISGA would promulgate regulations to guarantee fundamental human and legal rights in accordance with international conventions on human rights, thus providing this element of the security of the population.

With the end of military government steps would be taken to reverse the variety of forms of military control over civil life. For example, Israeli detention centers in the OT would close; prisoners still detained without trial would be released, and provision would be made to review the sentences against others. A tripartite body, consisting of Israeli, Palestinian and third party jurists, would review the sentences of prisoners in the expectation that some might have their period of incarceration shortened or ended. In addition, the review body might also accept appeals from persons who were tortured while in detention and provide financial compensation to them from a special fund provided by the Israeli government and concerned international parties.

During the transitional period, authority for the operation and enforcement of law and order in the OT would be gradually transferred from the Israeli military and police to the Palestinian ISGA. That transfer would entail, on a phased basis:

- Reconstruction of the Palestinian police force and court system in order to enforce law and order in accordance with the political decisions and the legal proceedings of the ISGA. A Palestinian-operated prison system would also be established during the transition period.

- Withdrawal of Israeli military forces from the municipal and village council areas in the OT, which would end day-to-day friction between soldiers and residents.

- Restriction of Israeli settlers to enforcing security within the perimeter of their settlements and the disbanding of settler militias.

- Enforcement of ISGA regulations and law over Israelis who enter areas administered by the ISGA.

- Creation of special Israeli-Palestinian police patrols to maintain security on the highways of the OT and at the entrance points between the OT and Israel, reinforced by international monitors.

- Maintenance of special Israeli-Palestinian guard units at vital installations, such as water-pumping stations, to protect against sabotage.

- Possible creation of a joint Israeli-Palestinian commission to examine apparent internal security threats, share information mutually and inform each other about steps to be taken.

Major investment in training Palestinian police and prison officers would be required, in order to reconstitute and expand the police force and to establish a prison system. The ISGA might seek international assistance to train officers and institute up-to-date management procedures. The size of the police force and its areas of responsibility and authority would be agreed upon in the negotiations. To establish authority, the police would need to bear specified arms and to be responsible for, *inter alia*, upholding criminal law, maintaining traffic control, and enforcing court orders. (Initially, Israel would issue handguns, following security clearances by the Israeli authorities.[28]) The police would also have gear for riot and crowd control. The ISGA would establish a hierarchy of command and control for area-wide police and for those operating within municipal and village areas. A Palestinian security apparatus would also be constructed during the interim period in order to prevent operations by indigenous groups designed to disrupt the accord. This security apparatus would probably have areas of coordination with Israeli counterpart agencies, especially during the initial years. That is a particularly sensitive issue, but vital for the long-term stability of the accord.

Reciprocal security arrangements would be required in order to respond to acts of violence by Israelis against Palestinians and by Palestinians against Israelis. The Israeli government and the ISGA would both have an interest in working out a specific security plan in order to prevent confusion concerning jurisdiction and to reduce the possibility of tension caused by such incidents. In the short term, Israel would maintain a security presence in the OT and would retain responsibility for handling security violations against Israelis or Israeli property. Such a presence could cause friction between Israel and the ISGA, and therefore careful delineation of areas of responsibility would be essential. Thorny questions of mixed political/security nature which might arise suggest the need for careful prior planning. For example: could Israeli security forces enter Palestinian homes and arrest persons on security charges or would such arrests be handled by the Palestinian police force on the basis of local court orders? Would a popular uprising against the ISGA justify Israeli military intervention? What steps might Israel take if a Palestinian kills a settler but the ISGA does not take legal action against the perpetrator? Once the ISGA establishes a police force and legal code, failure to resolve internal security threats, particularly against Israelis, could well constitute a violation of the agreement and compel Israel to intervene. Mechanisms for preventing and handling such crises should be established as early as possible in the interim period.

The Israeli government and the ISGA might establish a joint crisis monitoring center, involving Palestinian and Israeli security officials, in order to communicate quickly and directly and to preempt serious security violations. Third-parties might be invited to participate as facilitators, particularly in the early stages. A comprehensive security plan might include provisions that:

- Palestinians from the OT working in, traveling through or visiting Israel would be subject to Israeli law just as Israelis entering the OT would be subject to ISGA regulations.

- The ISGA police and security forces would be responsible for preventing Palestinian attacks against Israeli targets within its boundaries and for taking legal steps against any such actions.

- The Israeli government would be responsible for preventing attacks by Israelis against Palestinian targets.

- The ISGA would enact strong laws and impose stiff penalties for planning or carrying out acts of terror.

- The Israeli and ISGA authorities would exchange confidential information on imminent violent actions in order to help their counterparts maintain law and order; e.g. a planned operation by a Palestinian or an Israeli cell.

Many aspects of civil and economic life would have security implications. The issue of identity documents, for example, would be important. During the interim period, Palestinians would need to carry IDs with them as evidence of their residency and could be requested to show them to patrols on the highways. At first, they might hold Israeli IDs but by the end of the interim period, ISGA IDs might supplant Israeli IDs.

During the interim period, the principle of freedom of movement between the OT and Israel for economic and social purposes would be maintained. One suggestion for easing the transition is that the movement of any persons to the OT for permanent settlement might be banned. That would entail a freeze on all population movement, both Jewish and Arab. Just as no Israelis could move to the settlements in the OT, no Palestinians could return permanently from exile to the OT during the interim period. A joint Palestinian-Israeli commission could be established to resolve any disputes over implementation of the freeze and to allow for exceptions on humanitarian grounds. That form of mutual veto could be useful in the early stages of the interim period, while confidence is still being established.

The intricate relationship between security and the powers inherent in the ISGA would become apparent during the interim period. Meaningful self-rule could not be possible without the ISGA having specific forms of authority over territory. Without that authority, the ISGA would not be able to assure the security or livelihood of the residents. For example:

- Security of property: the notion of security cannot be limited to the physical protection of individuals but must include the security of one's property, home and land. Arbitrary takeovers, confiscations and invasions of property are direct attacks on a person's security.

- Security of investment: investments in public and private ventures cannot be secured without territorial security. Palestinians for example could not assume mortgages or business loans if Israel retains the power to confiscate land.

ISGA authority over land and individual Palestinians' right to security of their holdings would thus be imperative during the interim period. Many other needs — in areas of schooling, worship, and travel — can also only be met if specific territorial authority is vested in the ISGA. Otherwise, the interim period would only be a modified version of military occupation, not genuine self-rule.

The transitional period would be dynamic, involving phased shifts in authority over internal security and the repositioning of Israeli troops for maintaining external security. With the completion of each phase, the confidence of both sides in the security measures and environment would be enhanced. Specific stages would be written into the negotiation instrument in order to avoid misunderstandings and mechanisms to resolve disagreements would also be established in the accord.

The Long Term Status

As noted at the outset, this report is predicated on some form of Palestinian independence being agreed to in the final status. Many of the interim arrangements would differ markedly if permanent Israeli sovereignty was assumed as the end point of the second stage negotiations following the transitional period. The report assumes that agreement would be reached for either Palestinian or joint Jordanian-Palestinian sovereignty over the territories from which Israel would withdraw. Internal security within the Palestinian territory would be the sole responsibility of the Palestinian sovereign authority (PSA). International forces or observers might help guarantee the external security of the Palestinian state or the Palestinian portion of a Palestinian-Jordanian confederation. The long term Israeli-Palestinian resolution would take place in the context of peace treaties and security arrangements by Israel with Lebanon, Syria and Jordan, and the phased implementation of regional accords on arms limitation.

Israeli security has already been noted as grounded in the perceived strategic imbalance with the Arab world at large, not simply in the context of the OT. The need to meet those security fears underlines the importance of resolving the Israeli-Palestinian relationship in tandem with region-wide political agreements, security accords and arms control regimes. That need also reinforces the importance of establishing a territory-wide Palestinian-run authority on the grounds that such a central government will have strong incentives to enforce law and order. An integrated government leads to sensitivity to deterrence: a Palestinian government would not commit suicide by attacking its powerful neighbor.

Given the need to dispel mutual security fears and the importance of establishing a stable security regime, a final settlement will take place in three arenas: a regional Arab-Israeli security system, a trilateral Israeli-Palestinian-Jordanian security regime, and an internal security system for the West Bank and Gaza Strip. The comments which follow are illustrative of the forms such a system may take. The actual forms will emerge through negotiation and the development of a national Palestinian governing system.

The Regional Arab-Israeli Security Regime

The final status will be developed in the context of emerging peace and security accords between Israel and Syria and Lebanon, as outlined in the discussions of the negotiating and transitional phases. These peace treaties could be guaranteed by the UN or other international bodies and could be endorsed by the League of Arab States in order to ensure support from the other Arab governments. Key issues will include the status of Israeli early-warning monitors on Mount Hermon and the means to ensure verification of the demilitarized status of the Golan Heights and of a limited forces zone to the east. The implementation of negotiated security measures along the Lebanon-Israel border will also be an important element. They may include a UN-monitored demilitarized zone on the Lebanese side of the border and specified limitations to the forces and weapons that both Israel and Lebanon can place near the border. Full diplomatic relations will be established and the borders will be open for trade and tourism. In that context, Jewish citizens of Lebanon and Syria will have the right to decide where they want to live, and Palestinians living in Lebanon and Syria will have the right to visit their relatives and friends in Israel.

Regional accords will be particularly important in achieving a sense of stability for the final stage; they would link the Gulf states and Iraq into a regional security system along with the countries neighboring Israel. Internationally-monitored agreements on arms limitations, inspection of weapons installations and factories, and the elimination of nuclear and chemical weapons will be essential to a long-term agreement. The implementation of these arms control measures, if they take place in the context of diplomatic relations, trade, tourism, and shared water regimes, will be particularly secure.

Israel-Palestine-Jordan Security Regime

On the assumption that the OT will be linked closely to Jordan, a trilateral security system will need to be established among Israel, the Palestinian SGA and Jordan. That system might include provisions for[29]:

• A trilateral peace agreement including full diplomatic relations and a non-aggression pact.

• The establishment of mutually agreed security measures along the Israel-Jordan border, the Jordan-Palestine border, and the

Israel-Palestine border. Similar arrangements would be made with Egypt on the Gaza border.

- Arrangements would be made for citizens of each country to enter the other with agreed upon travel documents or IDs. Joint inspections at the crossing points might be instituted at the land, air and sea crossings with Jordan and Egypt.

- Jordan and Israel would sign mutual agreements limiting threatening deployments of forces near their borders. Neither country would deploy forces in the West Bank and Gaza Strip.

- Israel, Jordan and Palestine would be prohibited from allowing the deployment of foreign forces on their land, unless agreed upon by the other parties.

- Jordan and Palestine would be committed to refrain from joining defense alliances with external and regional powers.

- Israel and the US might sign a defense treaty with the sole objective to deter unprovoked attacks on Israel. The US might guarantee to come to the defense of any of the parties in the event of an attack by one on the other.

- Jordan, Palestine and Israel would join a regional arms control regime that would place specific limits on ground forces, air forces and ballistic missiles.

- Jordan, Palestine and Israel would formally adhere to the nuclear Non-Proliferation Treaty and the conventions against chemical and biological warfare. Their ban on weapons of mass destruction (nuclear, chemical and biological) would form an integral part of a regional arms agreement.

Israeli-Palestinian Security System

In the final stage, Palestinians would be concerned not only about their internal security but also about external security. The Palestinian sovereign authority (PSA) in the former OT would not have the military capacity to ensure external security, even in a confederation with Jordan, since it would remain essentially demilitarized and Jordanian troops would be prohibited from entering its territory.[30] Geostrategically, the Palestinian entity would be severely disadvantaged: Israel surrounds three sides of the West Bank and the Gaza Strip, patrols the Mediterranean waters, and controls transit between the West Bank and the Gaza Strip. Israeli armed forces could quickly cut the West Bank in two or reoccupy the Jordan

Valley, and all parts of the PSA's territory would be within range of Israeli artillery or missiles. The Palestinians would have to live in the context of that immense military disparity. Since a symmetrical security regime is not practical, measures to reassure the PSA against attacks from, or re-occupation by, Israel would be required.[31]

Attacks against the PSA could be launched either by Israeli groups or by the Israeli government. The former could include operations by irredentist militants who oppose the government's relinquishing land or who seek to provoke Palestinian retaliation and thereby disrupt the accord. The latter could include punitive cross-border attack by a military unit and actions by the security forces' hit squads against Palestinian leaders or bases. Israelis, too, would face the possibility of raids by irredentist Palestinians into Israel. In either country, elections might bring to power a government that would seek a pretext to cancel the peace agreement. Moreover, renewed conflict between Israel and an Arab government could provide the Israeli authorities with the excuse to invade the West Bank or Gaza. Therefore, a detailed security regime would be essential, which would include specification of treaty-breaking actions and methods to prevent or limit retaliation.

Provisions would be necessary for the maintenance of Israeli forces in the PSA as an integral part of Israel's external security system, including:

• Limitation of Israeli forces to one or two strategic positions in the Jordan Valley, as specified in negotiations with the PSA and Jordan. One Israeli strategist proposes that armored units be deployed 10-20 kilometers inside the PSA's territory, at the north and south ends of the valley, so they could quickly cut off the West Bank from the East in the event of an attack.[32] The positions would be leased from the Palestinian authority for a fixed time period and thus would not represent an extension of Israeli sovereignty. Their presence could be terminated if cooperative political relations were solidified and extensive regional arms control agreements were implemented. In that event, the reason for their presence — the risk of surprise attack from the East — would have been minimized.

• Maintenance of manned Israeli electronic early warning systems on highpoints on the West Bank in the early phases of the final accord, which would gradually shift to non-manned systems and might ultimately be replaced by satellite surveillance.

Arrangements would be made for limited periodic access to those sites for maintenance across agreed-upon routes.

- Specification that Israeli military forces in the PSA area would limit their activities to external security, with no intervention in domestic Palestinian affairs.

- Three sets of arrangements for Israel's continued access to the airspace over the West Bank and Gaza Strip: 1) provisions for commercial air traffic to ensure coordination of the air control systems given the small area and enable commercial planes from each country to overfly the other's territory on agreed routes; 2) provisions for security at the airports; 3) provisions for conditions under which the Israeli air force could continue to overfly the West Bank and Gaza Strip, including restrictions concerning the purpose, speed and altitude and continued prohibition of Arab airforces overflying the territories.

- Provisions for maintaining security in Jerusalem, assuming that the city is open to citizens from both Israel and Palestine-Jordan. Agreements on how to prevent hostile infiltration from one country to the other would be essential, possibly enforced by mixed police patrols and checkpoints.

- Provisions for periodic review of the security agreements and possible modification. If mutual threat perception diminishes, the terms would be altered to reflect the new reality.

Provisions would also be made for the demilitarization of the PSA; this might be achieved along the following lines:

- Demilitarization of the Palestinian area (West Bank and Gaza Strip) with explicit limits set on the location, the number and nature of forces and weapons. In practice, the PSA would have an armed police force responsible for internal and border security.[33]

- Maintenance by the PSA of a coast guard in the Mediterranean Sea off the Gaza Strip, with small patrol boats designed for search and rescue missions.

- Maintenance by the PSA of an air force to support the internal security mission, consisting of light reconnaissance craft and helicopters, based in Qalandiya and near Gaza City.

- Monitoring by Israel of border crossing points and the road connecting the West Bank and Gaza for security purposes only.

- Prevention of attacks against Israeli targets from Palestinian territories by the internal security forces of the PSA and punishment of perpetrators by the PSA. Israel would be responsible for prosecuting Palestinian guerrillas captured in its territory. If a joint crisis control center were established in the interim period, that center could deal with specific security threats and preempt cross-border attacks in hot-pursuit of either Palestinian or Israeli groups.

- Responsibility of the PSA's internal security forces for preventing armed groups from using Palestinian territories for attacks against Israel.

- Provision to disarm and disband Palestinian guerrilla forces and the Palestine Liberation Army units and absorb them into civilian life. Some individuals might serve in the police, or as prison guards, border inspectors, or security personnel for embassies.

Given the difficulty of achieving mutual security and building up trust between the Israeli and Palestinian authorities, international monitors could play a valuable role in the initial period of the final stage. They could help verify compliance with the accords and could facilitate cooperation between the parties to resolve disagreements. Their presence would underline the commitment of the international community to the long-term resolution of the Israeli-Palestinian conflict. Specific roles that third-party monitors might play include:

- Placement on the border with Israel in order to prevent or limit infiltration.[34]

- Provision of on-site teams or satellite-based mechanisms to verify security arrangements. On-site teams could inspect and help resolve violations; early warning stations could provide real-time data about force movements and maneuvers.

- Presence at border points to facilitate the smooth operation of security arrangements involving Israel, Jordan, the PSA and Egypt.

- Guarantee of the sovereignty, security and territorial integrity of the Palestinian entity against attack by Jordan as well as Israel.[35]

The legal expert Gidon Gottlieb notes that security and stability can be best maintained through a complex set of physical borders and functional lines of demarcation among Israel, Palestine and Jordan.[36] The political border and the line for redeployment of

Israeli military forces might not coincide. Political and economic borders could differ, particularly if a common market is achieved. Pragmatic solutions would be needed for major problems involving security, resources, and trade. Moreover, as the Israeli-Palestinian mutual threat perception diminishes with the passing of time, concern for the asymmetries in power might also diminish.[37] Security arrangements would become routinized and both sides would recognize their stake in maintaining law and order. Both sides would recognize that absolute security is impossible: security is always relative.

Once Arab-Israeli relations are no longer viewed in zero-sum terms, the state system can be stabilized in the Middle East and Israel can become an integral part of the region. In that sense, peace itself would provide security for Israelis and Palestinians. Despite military power and territorial control, Israel now has neither peace nor security. Full peace, normal relations, trade and economic interdependence would create a more secure situation. Land is tangible but does not ensure security; peace is intangible but brings tangible security.

Endnotes to Chapter II

1. "Framework" statement of 19 July 1991, *al-Fajr*, 23 September 1991, p. 9.
2. Gottlieb, p. 122. Dore Gold, a leading Israeli strategist and advisor to the Israeli delegation at Madrid, outlines Israel's defense doctrines in the light of the Gulf crisis in "Towards Middle East Peace Negotiations: Israeli Postwar Political-Military Options in an Era of Accelerated Changes," *Policy Focus* (Research Memorandum No. 16, The Washington Institute for Near East Policy, December 1991).
3. Ze'ev Schiff, "Israel after the War," *Foreign Affairs*, 70:2 (spring 1991), pp. 19-33.
4. Edy Kaufman, "Israeli Perceptions of the Palestinians' 'Limited Violence' in the *Intifada*," *Terrorism and Political Violence* (3:4, Winter 1991, pp. 1-38) comments perceptively on the reasons for Israelis' tendency to discount the seriousness of the relative move away from violence on the part of the Palestinians during the uprising. The cases cited in the text are taken from the *Jerusalem Post*, International Edition, 25 January 1992, p. 1; 1 February 1992, p. 3; and 8 February 1992, p. 3. *The New York Times*, 16 February 1992, reported the attack on Israeli soldiers.
5. Op-ed in *The New York Times*, 8 February 1992, p. 6.

6. Baruch Kimmerling, "Achieving a Comprehensive Agreement," background memorandum for American Academy of Arts and Sciences.

7. *Jerusalem Post*, 13 June 1992, p. 6.

8. Schiff, "Israel after the War," p. 29.

9. *News from Within*, VII:12, 5 December 1991, p. 7. The Israeli human rights center B'Tselem has documented official actions against Palestinians in numerous reports: for example, *The Interrogation of Palestinians During the Intifada: Ill-treatment, "Moderate Physical Pressure" or Torture?* (March 1991) and "Human Rights in the Occupied Territories During the War in the Persian Gulf," Information Sheet for January-February 1991.

10. Lesch, *Israel's Occupation*, p. 16, notes that only 34 of 800 policemen returned to their jobs after the June war in the Jerusalem district (which included Jericho and Ramallah) and so Israel recruited and trained replacements. By spring 1968, 282 Palestinians and 273 Israelis served in the West Bank police force. Shamgar, p. 444, states that in 1973 there were 320 Palestinian police and 240 Israeli police in the West Bank; in 1980, 377 Palestinian police and 214 Israeli police. However, all the prison wardens were Israeli: 250 in 1973 and 396 in 1980. Shalev, p. 92, using figures for both the West Bank and Gaza Strip, says that there were 825 Palestinian police in total, of whom only two were high ranking officers and fourteen were lower rank officers.

11. Shalev, p. 90, notes that military courts handle "offences not connected with security, such as traffic, customs, bribery, licensing, trials of shepherds, foreign currency, etc." Zvi Hadar, "The Military Courts," in Shamgar, pp. 171-216, details their procedures; Appendix C (pp. 492-5) includes a military order of 1970 on the military courts. Their operation and the changes in the legal system are analyzed in Emma Playfair, "The Legal Aspects of the Occupation: Theory and Practice," in Aruri, pp. 101-196.

12. Lesch, *Israel's Occupation*, pp. 17-19; Playfair, pp. 120-123; George Emile Bisharat, *Palestinian Lawyers and Israeli Rule* (University of Texas Press, 1989). In Shamgar, Ya'akov Meron describes the operation of Muslim and Christian "Religious Courts in the Administered Territories," pp. 353-366, and Drori, pp. 253-55 mentions that Israel set up a municipal court for Bethlehem, Beit Jala and Beit Sahour in 1976, which handled violations of municipal by-laws and regulations within municipal boundaries; the municipalities collected the fines imposed by the Palestinian-staffed court.

13. *The Jerusalem Post*, 11 January 1992; the stabbing came after Hamas disrupted Faisal Husayni's presentation in Tulkarm.

14. Ann M. Lesch, "Palestinians in Kuwait," *Journal of Palestine Studies*, XX:4, summer 1991, pp. 50-53.

15. *Article 74*, no. 1, 11 November 1991; and *Information Sheet: Update September-October 1991*, B'Tselem, Jerusalem. Subsequently, the government argued that the court ruling only applied to persons who had arrived before June 1990 and issued expulsion orders to additional wives and children, but none have been expelled forcibly.

16. Suggested to the author by Edy Kaufman, human rights professor at Hebrew University, 7 January 1992.

17. "Nowhere to Go: Palestinians in Kuwait," *News from Middle East Watch*, October 1991; *News from Within*, 5 December 1991, p. 12, says only 30,000 Palestinians came to the West Bank and 7000 to Gaza from Kuwait.

18. See, for example, UN Security Council resolution 726 (6 January 1992) which, in condemning Israel's plan to deport twelve Palestinians, "reaffirms the applicability of the Fourth Geneva Convention of 12 August 1949 to all the Palestinian territories occupied by Israel since 1967, including Jerusalem."

19. Suggested by Riad Malki, professor at Bir Zeit University, in a discussion with the Academy's study group, 18 July 1991.

20. Suggested in background memo by Kaufman and Awad.

21. Interview in *Jerusalem Post*, 2 November 1991, p. 4.

22. The Unified Leadership for the National Uprising (UNLU) has already issued such condemnations, and has also ordered that no one should wear masks when among Palestinians, only in conflicts with the army. When an Israeli girl was stabbed to death by a resident of Gaza on May 24, 1992, Faisal Husayni and other leaders quickly condemned killing civilians (*al-Fajr*, 1 June 1992, p. 15).

23. The Unified National Leadership has already attempted to end extra-judicial killings, as leaflet #80 (1 March 1992) indicates: "The UNL appeals to the strike forces to heed the orders regarding the elimination of collaborators — to refer to higher ranks in the organization before making the decision of physical elimination. The criticism which the national leadership expressed regarding the elimination of the three collaborators in Kafr Ra'i (Jenin area) does not at all mean that we absolve them of guilt. The criticism comes from concern for the civilized image of our people. In these matters, we must act cautiously and justly." Quotes in *News from Within*, VIII: 3/4 (March-April 1992), pp. 28-29. That call was repeated in leaflet #83, which also sought to end inter-factional conflict (*al-Fajr*, 15 June 1992, p. 8) and by the head of the Palestinian delegation (*al-Fajr*, 1 June 1992, p. 5).

24. Suggested initially by Jerome Segal in *Creating the Palestinian State: A Strategy for Peace* (Chicago: Lawrence Hill Books, 1989), pp. 67, 92. Segal argues that, even though Israel's fears are irrational, they are "a very crucial national security fact" that the Palestinians must address. Segal also stresses (p. 74) Israelis' fear of terrorism: terrorism raises the

specter of the Holocaust, which denied the right of Jews to exist as individuals and as a people. Terror, by denying the existence of limits in the forms and objects of violence, similarly appears to deny the right of the Israeli state and people to exist.

25. Ze'ev Schiff, *Security for Peace: Israel's Minimal Security Requirements in Negotiations with the Palestinians* (Washington, D.C.: The Washington Institute for Near East Policy, Policy Paper #15, 1989), pp. 55-57. Schiff assumes that, even under optimal circumstances, Israel would keep troops at the north and south ends of the Jordan Valley and in the southern part of the Gaza Strip, abutting Sinai. He suggests, however, that Israel might not need to keep early warning stations in the central West Bank, stating that ground stations inside Israel and airborne stations could be sufficient.

26. Gold, p. 6.

27. Shalev, p. 86.

28. Suggested by Gershon Baskin in his peace proposal, p. 6.

29. Several of the following ideas are based on Yair Evron, "Israeli-Palestinian-Jordanian Security Relations: The Idea of a Security Zone," *Emerging Issues*, Occasional Paper no. 3, May 1990, American Academy of Arts and Sciences, p. 36.

30. Ahmad S. Khalidi, "Middle East Security: Arab Threat Perceptions, Peace, and Stability," *Emerging Issues*, Occasional Paper no. 3 (May 1990), American Academy of Arts and Sciences, p. 3.

31. It is interesting to note that Walid Khalidi in *Foreign Affairs* (1978) feared that a totally demilitarized Palestinian state would be "a eunuch" (p. 703) or a "sitting duck" (p. 713), tempting Israel to attack. He provided hypothetical figures for minimal Palestinian air and ground forces that would be needed to "curb adventurism across the border into Israel" (p. 704) while maintaining "eminently credible" deterrence vis-à-vis Israel.

32. Evron, p. 44. Heller, p. 141, suggests that a permanent border change be made at the north end of the Jordan valley, so that Israel would control a zone 10 kilometers deep. He also suggests the permanent incorporation of the Latrun salient and the post-1967 Jerusalem-to-Tel Aviv highway into Israel, indicating that some reciprocal concession might be possible by Israel, possibly the shift of part of the Little Triangle (a concentration of Arab villages) to the Palestinian state.

33. Heller, p. 138 and Heller and Nusseibeh, who suggest (pp. 67-68) that the Palestinian army would have three brigades (one in Gaza) with personal weapons, armored cars, light mortars, and communications and transport equipment. The army would not have tanks, artillery, missiles or fortifications. See also the English analyst Valerie Yorke, "A Two-State Solution: Security, Stability and the Superpowers," in Hudson, especially pp. 179-184.

34. Yasir Arafat suggested that as early as 1978, according to the *The New York Times*, 22 November 1978, cited in Yorke, p. 180.
35. Proposed by Palestinians in Moughrabi *et al.*, p. 48.
36. Gottlieb, pp. 120-21.
37. Khalil Shikaki, "Palestinian Security Requirements and the Political Settlement," background memorandum.

III

Economic and Resource Issues

Both Israelis and Palestinians stand to benefit from a stable and prosperous economy in the West Bank and Gaza. The transition from occupation to self-government and ultimately to some form of independence will be smoother for the Palestinians and less threatening to the Israelis if a viable and vibrant economy is created and maintained. For political self-rule to be substantive, the Palestinians must, of course, have control over their economic institutions and resources. Given the high degree of integration or virtual annexation of the OT economy to Israel's economy since 1967, the transitional period will require a complex process of reshaping the economic relationship on the basis of mutual benefits. There will be a simultaneous process of disengagement, restructuring and institution building.

That multifaceted process involving Israel and the OT will occur in the context of altered Israeli relations with the Arab world. Commercial flows will develop to become open and multidimensional, benefiting all parties. The launching of cooperation in augmenting regional resources such as water and electricity will enhance economic growth and reinforce regional diplomatic and security relations. The very process of establishing Palestinian self-rule will thereby benefit Israel as well as the Palestinians. By relinquishing the OT as a key in normalizing relations with the Arab world, Israel will achieve important gains in access to Arab markets and vital resources.

The Status Quo

Israeli Constraints on the OT Economy

Palestinian economic life under occupation operates under severe constraints. The Israeli government controls the basic resources and infrastructure: land, water, electricity, roads and communication systems. All policy-making and long-term planning are in the hands of Israeli officials and the economy has been molded at many levels to serve Israel's interests. The disparity in GNP between Israel and the OT is also pronounced: Israel's $45 billion GNP contrasts with $2 billion for the OT. Income differentials are approximately $1000 per capita in the OT, $2000 in Jordan and $7000 in Israel.[1] While this discussion does not purport to detail all facets of economic life, it will highlight several key aspects, including:

Policy making: All policy-making and long-term planning are in the hands of Israeli officials.[2] The Israeli-established Higher Planning Council for the OT controls all spatial development, which is oriented toward expanding Israeli settlements while constricting the growth of Palestinian towns and villages. An all-Israeli board reviews Palestinian appeals against planning decisions. The military government also restricts the authority of municipal and village councils to regulate infrastructure development within their limits and frequently denies requests for building permits.

Land: The military government has barred land registration by Palestinians since 1967 and forbids Palestinians not currently residing in the territories from inheriting land. The military government must approve all land transactions and controls the land registers. Notification of expropriation can be oral and appeal to local courts is prohibited; the only recourse is to the Israeli High Court or to an advisory military objections committee. The Israeli government has taken control over six categories of land which comprise approximately half of the West Bank and a third of the Gaza Strip:[3]

a) all land that Jordan and Egypt designated as state land;

b) land owned by persons who were outside the OT in June 1967, termed absentee or "abandoned" land;

c) private land requisitioned for military use, e.g. army camps;

d) private land whose access is denied, "closed areas" for military firing ranges, training grounds and general "security" zones;

e) private land requisitioned for public use such as roads, utilities and parks;

f) land where the registration process was incomplete in 1967 and which the military government has designated "public" even if the occupant possesses tax records or sale documents; one third of the West Bank and 20 percent of the Gaza Strip are affected, particularly in relation to *miri* land (originally owned by the Ottoman ruler but privatized by Jordan in 1953) and *mawat* ("dead", waste land used by villages for pasture and future growth but not registered as private property).

Water:[4] Water use is restricted by limits placed on Palestinian access to water and by its competitive use by Israeli settlements and within Israel itself:

- The military government controls all water resources in the OT, prohibits drilling new wells or deepening old wells without its permission (which is only granted for domestic use, not industry or agriculture), fixes pumping quotas, and denies Palestinians the use of wells in expropriated or closed areas.

- The Palestinian population on the West Bank grew by 84 percent since 1967 but water allotted for domestic use only increased 20 percent and no increase was allowed for agriculture and industry. A mere 6 percent of the 1.7 million dunums of land cultivated by Palestinians on the West Bank is irrigated (the same amount as 1967). In 1990 Palestinians were allotted only 17 percent of the West Bank's ground water, which derives from aquifers on the eastern and western slopes of the mountain ridge; 83 percent is used within Israel or by Israeli settlements in the West Bank.

- The approximately 100,000 settlers on the West Bank use 160 mcm yearly, 20 percent of the water resources (1990), and irrigate 69 percent of the 563,000 dunums cultivated. In contrast, only 137 mcm water was allocated to the 1 million Palestinians in 1989: each settler received 1,600 cm that year and each Palestinian received 127 cm. Settlements drill deep bore (artesian) wells, particularly in the eastern aquifer that drains into the Jordan Valley, and consequently dry up nearby Arab springs.

- Two-thirds of West Bank water resources are currently diverted for use inside Israel (1990), providing a third of Israel's total water needs.[5] Despite reduced levels in the aquifers, pumping on the coastal plain has remained high.

- The Gaza Strip relies on fresh water from an aquifer that partly flows under Israel.[6] Its Palestinian residents irrigate 45 percent of the agricultural land, using 90 percent of the water for irrigation. The aquifer is only replenished by 60 percent yearly due to overpumping by Palestinian farmers, pumping from new wells for settlements in the Gaza Strip, pumping from wells inside Israel that serve the Israeli National Water Carrier, and dams on Wadi Gaza inside Israel that prevent its water from flowing into the Strip. Those Israeli wells east of Gaza impact negatively on the quality and quantity of water in the Strip. The resulting intrusion of seawater into the aquifer has raised salinity to levels that damage agriculture and contaminate drinking water, causing serious health problems. Restrictions have been placed on pumping by Palestinians but not by Israelis inside the Strip or along the border. On average, Palestinians have access to 200 cm per capita water yearly, not even 10 percent of the settlers' share.[7]

Electricity: the Palestinians' Jerusalem Electricity Company continues to operate in the central West Bank but must buy all its power from Israel.[8] The military government forbids West Bank municipalities from repairing electricity stations that were established before 1967 or installing new ones. The few remaining local generators buy their fuel from Israel. Gaza Strip electricity is provided entirely by Israel.

Agriculture: Agriculture provides a quarter of the gross domestic product and employs 31 percent of the Palestinian labor-force on the West Bank; for Gaza the figures are 18 percent of the GDP and 19 percent of the work force. The agricultural sector faces severe difficulties. In addition to the loss of land and restrictions on water use, farmers are limited in the amount and kinds of agriculture, livestock and fishing and in access to technology and training:

- The military government requires farmers to obtain a permit to plant fruit or citrus trees or (since 1983) vegetables. No permits to plant citrus in Gaza have been given since 1967, resulting in a severe drop in the quantity and quality of output.[9] Restrictions on planting have lowered production in the Gaza Strip of melons, onions, grapes, almonds, and olives. Access to three-quarters of the fishing area off the Strip is blocked on security grounds.

- Crops are restricted that might compete with Israeli produce, whereas Israeli farmers can sell freely in the OT. No permits are given to Gaza farmers to grow mangoes and avocados, which are profitable in Israel; strawberries are encouraged, which do not compete with Israeli farmers . Until mid-1991, all produce sold to Israel had to receive a special permit and most produce could only be sold through an Israeli marketing monopoly.

- Government agricultural research stations and extension programs have been reduced markedly since the mid-1970s.[10] West Bank farmers have few opportunities to learn about optimal planting methods, seeds, and uses of fertilizers and pesticides. No university level agricultural program was permitted until 1986. Labels on Israeli seeds and pesticides are in Hebrew rather than Arabic, which compounds the risk of improper use and potential crop failure.

- Farmers cannot upgrade their production by controlling the entire process. Israeli companies are not allowed to sell tissue culture for dates to Palestinian farmers, to provide the knowhow for fish fingerlings, or to sell dairy cows and chicks for breeding. Palestinians therefore buy cows and chicks on the black market, which is costly and poses quality problems. (UNDP received Israeli permission in 1991 to establish a chicken hatchery in the OT, after a three year wait.)

Industry: Industry comprises only 7.7 percent of the West Bank GDP and 13.7 percent of the Gaza Strip GDP, whereas construction contributes 16.8 percent and 21.2 percent, respectively, and services account for 51.1 percent and 46.5 percent.[11] The military government has not allowed industries that might compete with Israeli factories to be established, whereas Israeli manufactured goods sell without restriction in the OT. In the Gaza Strip, industrialists have been prevented from building factories to produce juice concentrate, can sardines, or mix cement. Sub-contracting by Israeli firms has been encouraged, thereby enhancing dependence on the Israeli economy since the Palestinians earn piece-work wages and profits accrue to the Israeli firms. Gaza subcontracting includes cane furniture, plastics, clothing, and woven rugs.[12] Most factories are small scale, largely using members of a family; only 20 firms in the West Bank and 10 in Gaza hire more than 50 workers. Pre-1967 factories in Gaza for bottling soft-drinks and in the West Bank for olive oil, soap, cigarettes, sweets, dairy product processing, and tissues continue to operate, relying on local or Israeli raw materials. Shoes, marmalade, pickles and vegetable canning take place on a small scale, but few factories can process chicken, meat or frozen foods, especially since permits were rarely given to form industrial cooperatives until 1991. Fruit and vegetable packing houses rely on Israeli containers and lack adequate refrigeration for storage. (Israel did permit a fishing cooperative in Gaza to buy a refrigerated truck and construct an ice-packing house, in the early 1980s.)

Trade: Eighty percent of OT exports are sold to or through Israel and 91 percent of OT imports enter from or through Israel.[13] An Israeli marketing officer serves as liaison between the Israeli citrus,vegetable and poultry boards and the OT agricultural offices; the officer issues the permits to export to Israel. Specific characteristics include:

- Half of OT agricultural produce is sold to or through Jordan: a limited number of trucks receive permits from Israel to cross the two bridges, where they often face long delays that can damage the fruit and produce; selective banning of exports from particular areas is a common punitive measure.

- The OT imports from Israel virtually all consumer goods; subsidized Israeli cooperatives often undersell local producers in foods such as eggs and poultry.

- Israel generally limits sales of agricultural products from the OT to Israel to non-competitive produce or low-price produce for canning and juice factories. Sub-contractors must provide their output to the Israeli firm.

- Marketing abroad through Israel was strictly controlled, until late 1991, by Israeli monopolies and restricted to non-competitive items and locations. Since the late 1980s, a limited exception has been made for produce sales to western Europe, after the European Community induced Israel to allow OT producers to sell directly to European markets. Barter deals to eastern Europe for Gaza citrus ended in 1975, but barter continued for certain West Bank fruits through the 1980s. The Palestinian exporters must pay for costly security inspections at the Ashdod port and Ben Gurion airport and must use high-price Israeli load agents; delays and damage in transit can reduce the value of the exports.[14]

- Internal limitations in marketing, including the lack of up-to-date information and management systems as well as security restrictions on movement, hamper internal and external trade. Businessmen have difficulty moving raw materials, products, and funds from one city to another, and workers often cannot reach their jobs.[15]

Labor: The Palestinian labor force depends heavily on work inside Israel. Despite reductions in labor during the intifada and the Gulf crisis, approximately a third of OT workers are employed in Israel.[16] The proportion is highest for Gaza laborers.

Credit: Israel closed all the Arab and international banks in 1967, leaving the population without financial institutions that could provide loans for agricultural or industrial development. Israel allowed the Palestine bank in Gaza to reopen in 1981, but limited its transactions to Israeli currency. The Nablus branch of the Cairo Amman Bank reopened in 1986, using the Jordanian dinar, which remains legal tender in the West Bank; but residents of East Jerusalem can open accounts only in Israeli currency, no deposits can come from abroad, and the military government must approve all loans.[17] The OT is affected by fluctuations in both Israeli and Jordanian currencies: inflationary effects are magnified, since no financial institutions cushion the impact. (See below on recent efforts to establish financial institutions.)

Tariffs: An important drain on the OT economy is caused by tariffs that the Israeli government collects on imports into Israel which are then resold to the OT by Israeli merchants: Israel gains $100 million annually from those tariffs. If credited to the OT budget, they would double current government expenditure in the OT.[18]

Arab boycott: The Arab ban on goods from Israel also restricts OT sales since Jordan refuses to import OT goods that contain Israeli raw materials or are packaged in Israeli cans or cartons. That prevents the OT from exporting manufactured goods to the Arab world. Such exports are limited to cut stone for construction and agricultural produce, for which permits must be obtained from Jordan's Agricultural Ministry via the Palestine Department of the Foreign Ministry. Political shifts also hurt OT commerce: the fall of the Shah in 1979 ended the export of Gaza citrus to Iran; Saudi Arabia blocked goods shipped via Jordan during and after the Gulf crisis.

Palestinian Efforts to Develop Their Economy

Palestinian efforts to improve their economic life are severely constrained by Israeli occupation policies. The efforts have been undermined by Israeli actions that are justified on security grounds: seizures of farmland or orchards, closures of factories, curfews on villages, travel bans against merchants and vehicles, and confiscatory-level taxes and fees. Nonetheless, the OT's economic problems are exacerbated by indigenous weaknesses, such as limited business, management and technical skills, low level of capitalization of businesses, and duplication of produce and products.

Since the intifada began, Palestinians have sought to develop a new paradigm that would not merely permit short-term survival but would lead to long-term development.[19] They seek to emphasize production over consumption and to establish their own priorities for development, rather than react to externally-generated projects. The intifada helped to empower local communities and to establish local and territory-wide institutional structures outside the control of the military government. Four trends are particularly evident: first, efforts to create jobs in the OT; second, enhanced research and outreach in agriculture, industry and trade; third, the establishment of credit institutions; and fourth, attempts to build grassroots and coordinating economic institutions.

Job Creating Efforts

The first trend stresses the importance of creating jobs in the OT. That effort predates the Gulf crisis and reflects the perspective of intifada activists that local agriculture and industry must be developed as alternatives to Israeli products. Intifada leaflets call for the boycott of Israeli goods when indigenous substitutes are available, urge landlords to reduce rent, and exhort businessmen to raise salaries and not fire workers. Although gross national income dropped in 1988 and 1989 and local industries operated at less than half capacity, Palestinian economists argue that the economic boycott began to have a positive impact on the level of investment in the private sector in 1989-90.[20] The impact was particularly pronounced in agriculture, where the cultivation of vegetables and fruit and amount of animal husbandry increased markedly, resulting in a corresponding drop in the consumption of Israeli vegetables, fruit, eggs and milk. Inexperience in farming and overproduction of certain crops caused some failures. Moreover, curfews imposed by the army caused considerable damage: crops rotted in the fields and chickens died when they could not be fed. The army also uprooted trees,[21] confiscated land, cut water allocations, blocked transport, and destroyed farm machinery. Palestinian-called strikes also hampered these economic efforts.

The Gulf crisis, which caused substantial disruptions in production, trade and remittances, increased the emphasis on economic self-empowerment. Factories maintained extended work days, shops and restaurants remained open longer hours, and the number of strike days per month was reduced. The Israeli government signaled in 1991 a willingness to relax restrictions on licensing businesses and cooperatives, apparently in recognition of the economic crisis facing the OT community. Palestinian businesses are taking advantage of that relaxation to license previously unregistered businesses, to establish new firms, and to create agricultural and industrial cooperatives. Few new firms, however, have been approved and political criteria continue to dominate Israel's decisions to approve or reject applications.

Nonetheless, the fact that the OT has never been self-supporting must be considered by Palestinian economic planners. Before the Gulf crisis GDP was only half GNP, the large difference coming from wages earned in Israel and from remittances from Palestinian family members working abroad, according to the Israeli economist Ruth Klinov. Palestinians give priority to expanding domestic production and employment, since their independence is compromised when their incomes and work conditions are governed by foreign countries. But their efforts must be informed by knowledge of the structural characteristics and limitations of the domestic economy. Such baseline research remains limited.

Technical Research

The second trend emphasizes the importance of undertaking research on the feasibility of economic projects and expanding outreach to farmers, businessmen and industrialists. The OT has lacked baseline data, feasibility studies, management and marketing plans, all of which are vital in order to establish new product lines and to expand or modify existing ones. Israel for its part restricts Palestinians from collecting the necessary data and conducting surveys, and the OT lacks a radio or TV station by which such information could be disseminated widely and efficiently.[22] Palestinian agronomists emphasize that analyses are needed of soil content and water salinity in order to assess the suitability of particular plots of land for certain crops. Farmers need to be educated in the treatment of crop diseases. Poultry hatcheries, breeding cows, and tissue culture for dates are vital for self-sustained agricultural development. Private research institutions, universities and cooperatives try to fill the gaps in knowledge and production, but lack adequate funds, expertise and authority. Examples of current efforts include:

- **Quality-control agencies** for pharmaceuticals and olive oil, in order to upgrade and standardize the products and thereby enhance consumer confidence and marketability. Manufacturers submit voluntarily to the tests and grading undertaken by laboratories, but the absence of governmental authority hampers their operation.

- **Agricultural committees**: The Palestinian Agricultural Relief Committee (PARC), for example, based in Jericho, operates experimental stations and provides technical advice on crops. In 1990, PARC employed 45 engineers (including 7 female agronomists); worked with 60 village level committees and 33 women's cooperatives, which received seeds, rabbits, and chickens; and made 2,500 extension visits to 122 villages. PARC also distributed 500,000 vegetable seedlings produced in its own nursery and operated rabbit farms in Beit Jala and Ramallah. Smaller scale operations by the Technical Center for Agricultural Services assisted local agricultural committees and the Union of Agricultural Work Committees distributed vegetable seedings as well as egg-laying chickens and gamehens.[23] Each of these agricultural efforts is tied to one of the four different political factions active in the OT.

- **Environmental research**: The numerous groups working on environmental research and outreach include two in Gaza — Environmental Protection Agency and Gaza Environmental Program — which seek to monitor the water crisis in the Strip.[24] Bir Zeit University's Center for Environmental and Occupational Health Sciences (CEOHS) monitors Ramallah area water on contract from the Ramallah water authority and has launched a campaign to train farmers in the use of pesticides. The Palestine Hydrology Group surveyed West Bank springs during 1987-89 and now assists farmers to improve yield from their springs, build rain-fed cisterns, and purify water. The Education for Awareness and Involvement Project is publishing booklets on health and environmental issues and encouraging community clean-ups.

- **The Applied Research Institute**, Jerusalem (ARIJ) grew out of the efforts by agricultural specialists in Beit Sahour to distribute seeds, seedlings, fertilizer, and irrigation pipes and to provide free expertise to farmers during the opening months of the intifada.

ARIJ has published bulletins concerning the control of diseases in tomatoes and bees, the management of goats, and the production of hydroponic fodder.[25]

Credit Institutions

The third trend emphasizes establishing, strengthening and expanding credit institutions in the OT.[26] Four non-profit shareholder companies have opened in Jerusalem in the last five years, registered with the Israeli Ministry of Industry and Trade. (One of them was established under UNRWA auspices.) Each is capitalized at $2-3.5 million and gives loans for agricultural, industrial or infrastructure projects. The Arab Development and Credit Company (ADCC), for example, has provided about 600 loans at $8-9000 each for poultry, greenhouses, irrigation and wells. The Economic Development Group focuses on industries and workshops, and the new Technical Development Committee provides share capital to entrepreneurs. The companies only have 65 percent repayment rates due to both the Gulf crisis and the absence of effective courts and police by which they can enforce collection. The credit institutions require substantial external funding, largely from the European Community, both as start-up capital and as a cushion until the repayment rate improves. Their capacity is limited: none can accept deposits (unlike a bank) and their loans are minute in relation to need.

Community Groups and Coordinating Bodies

The fourth trend emphasizes efforts to link community groups to OT-wide coordinating bodies. Local cooperatives have served as useful means to pool resources, capital, expertise, and labor, and to spread profit and loss. Twenty per cent of farm families in the West Bank belong to cooperatives, and housing cooperatives helped people construct homes in the absence of a housing bank. But the efforts remain limited and fragmented. Community groups that promote backyard vegetable gardens served an emergency purpose during the intifada and demonstrated the importance of indigenous self-help, but had a greater symbolic value than practical impact. Thus, efforts have been made to establish OT-wide coordinating committees in agriculture, industry and tourism in order to coordinate policies and programs in both the West Bank and Gaza Strip. They incorporate the major political factions into their membership and also include leading professionals in those economic fields, thereby attempting to balance representation and technical effectiveness. They also seek to coordinate the distribution and investment of international funds from the Arab world as well as the European Community.

Palestinians also participated in elections for six municipal chambers of commerce in the OT and Jerusalem in 1991-92. One of the chambers had held an election in 1973, but the others had not reelected their administrative councils since 1964, prior to the Israeli occupation. Palestinians saw the elections as an opportunity to rejuvenate the trade and business community and to address and publicize economic concerns.[27]

The presence of numerous community groups, cooperatives, and chambers of commerce emphasizes the fragmented nature of economic activities. The coordinating committees remain rudimentary: some Palestinians fear they will overcentralize and control economic activities, whereas others fear they will not be strong enough to reduce unnecessary duplication and competition. The politicization of economic life and technocratic functions is also a reality. However, under the conditions of occupation, Palestinians believe that maintaining diffuse networks of institutions may be necessary in order to spread and minimize risk.

Arab and International Funds

Foreign financial assistance to residents of the OT has taken widely varying forms. Medical and social relief has been channeled through UNRWA and charitable agencies. Arab and Palestinian assistance has tended to support particular political groups or sought to buy the political loyalty of leading individuals. Such assistance, even if given to cooperatives or for income-generating projects, was not given primarily in the expectation that the project would be economically viable; but rather, to help the population remain steadfast (*sumud*) on the land.

By the mid-1970s, European and American aid agencies — both governmental and private — sought to minimize the relief and welfare component in their programs and sought instead avenues for long-term economic and social development in the OT. Non-governmental agencies can be relatively experimental in their approach, while governments acting on their own have been cautious politically. The USAID program, which channeled its funds through American PVOs, accepted Israeli conditions that the military government approve all projects, whether in education, social services, infrastructure, agriculture, or industry.[28] The UN Development Programme even agreed to fund only programs run by the Israeli government, notably the social affairs and health departments. As a result, Israel could alter the priorities of the donor through its approval process. Sara Roy, an economic development specialist, reports that USAID wanted to place half its projects in agriculture and industry, but the approval rate for them was so low that only a third of all projects were implemented in those areas. Conversely, Israeli approvals shifted the balance toward infrastructure and social service: those projects totaled half, instead of the one-third, of all projects that USAID had intended. The military government has generally rejected projects that involve land reclamation, new industrial cooperatives, indigenous research institutes, local credit institutions, independent electrical power structures, the development of alternative water resources, and the purchase of certain agricultural and industrial machinery. Although the aid given has been beneficial at the microlevel, Roy argues, it lacks an integrated framework and cannot support activities that would create greater self-sufficiency and reduce structural ties to Israel.

European governments and private voluntary organizations have not agreed to submit all projects to Israeli clearance and therefore have managed to circumvent some of the restrictions. The Spanish government, for example, has provided funds through the European Community to the Palestine Bank in Gaza for agricultural loans. Moreover, in 1987-88 the EC made its preferential trade agreement with Israel conditional on allowing OT produce to transit directly to Europe on terms similar to those applying to Israeli farmers. That enabled the OT to export 2200 tons of citrus and 89 tons of eggplants to the EC in 1988, which jumped to 5000 tons and 500 tons, respectively, in 1989. EC economic aid also doubled, from $6.6 million in 1990 to $13.2 million in 1992 and was supplemented by a special appropriation of $73.8 million to ease the impact of the Gulf crisis. US economic aid has averaged $12 million yearly (1990-92), for an overall $130 million aid from the US government between 1975 and 1992, excluding food aid and Washington's share of UN-RWA operations.[29]

Most foreign agencies work directly with indigenous Palestinian institutions. But externally-imposed priorities can distort the aid process. Most importantly, relying on external funds limits the need and will to mobilize local resources and ensure that projects are economically viable. Now that Palestinians are enhancing their own expertise in development issues, they are in a stronger position to assert their priorities and to influence the decisions made by foreign donors. Nonetheless, the fundamental constraints placed by the military authorities on Palestinian institutional development limit the potential effectiveness of foreign aid under current circumstances.

Negotiating Phase

Multilateral and bilateral negotiations are apt to be protracted in relation to economic and resource issues as well as political and security concerns. The basic requirements for a meaningful ISGA will involve the reduction in Israeli control over the allocation of economic resources and trade, the acquisition of sufficient authority by the ISGA to begin to create an independent economy, and a move toward ISGA control over the land as an integral part of its economic powers. Regional economic and resource issues are also an important part of the multilateral negotiations, particularly concerning water sharing and ending the Arab boycott of trade with Israel.

Confidence-Building Measures

If the Fourth Geneva Convention were applied to the OT, a wide range of measures that harm economic life would cease, notably land confiscation, the establishment of settlements, the imposition of punitive taxes, and collective punishments such as curfews, restrictions on travel and commerce, and the closure of universities. Those changes would introduce an element of security and predictability into economic life in the OT and encourage economic activities by local entrepreneurs.

Even without a formal Israeli pledge to apply the Convention to the OT, Israeli confidence-building measures would indicate that the government was serious about ameliorating socio-economic conditions and starting to alter the economic relationship between Israel and the OT. Short-term actions that would reduce hardships could include:

• Lifting travel restrictions,
• Stopping raids against businesses and homes to collect taxes and fines,
• Ending curfews so farmers can tend crops and orchards and businessmen can operate shops and factories.

Measures which would help stabilize the economy of the OT can be taken independent of the negotiating process. They would quickly benefit the Palestinian economy and assist Israeli merchants and employers. Further, these steps would reduce tension in the OT and indicate that some positive benefits might result from negotiations, thus bolstering the credibility of the negotiating process. Israeli officials have hinted that they might moderate certain travel restrictions placed on businessmen and reduce or eliminate some taxes and fees.[30] Moreover, licensing of indigenous businesses has been simplified recently and the recent restriction of Israeli marketing cartels should ease access for Palestinian products to Israeli and foreign markets.

Policy Changes

Israel's intent would be indicated by introducing substantive reorientations in policy-making and economic practices in the OT that would set the stage for the interim period. Such measures include:

• **Budget:** Publish the budget of the civil administration (revenue and expenditure).

• **Planning:** Allow municipalities to regain policy-making authority within their boundaries in order to plan improvements in housing, water supply, social welfare, education and services for businesses and industry that would be implemented during the interim period.

• **Land:** Renew the process of registering private land, and undertake a joint Palestinian-Israeli survey of the current status and use of the categories of land mentioned earlier.

• **Water:** Undertake a joint Palestinian-Israeli assessment of current water use and anticipated needs in Israel and the OT for domestic, agricultural and industrial purposes, based on the principle of equity and taking into account the overall scarcity of water.

• **Worker benefits:** Compute the funds deducted by employers in Israel from Palestinian wages that are allocated to the Israeli labor federation (Histadrut) and the National Insurance Institute, and ensure that they are spent on worker benefits, and prepare for their allocation to the OT's General Federation of Trade Unions (GFTU) and the Palestinian social service office during the interim period.

- **Credit:** Reopen the former banks and license credit institutions in the OT in order to provide loans to farmers, businessmen, industrial firms, and cooperatives in order to stimulate the economy.

- **Tax:** Restructure the tax system to reduce OT taxes to the level in Israel[31] and allocate to the OT administration all taxes and fees levied on OT residents.

Palestinian Efforts

During negotiations, the Palestinian community in the OT would continue its fourfold effort to strengthen the local economy, improve technical research and outreach, deepen credit institutions, and coordinate economic institutions. There will be political struggles within the Palestinian community for control over key institutions and over the anticipated economic planning process as well as for grassroots support. Considerable duplication of effort and competition among political groups are likely, which could skew economic priorities. The internal debate will continue on how best to decrease economic dependency on Israel and how to create the bases for economic growth, particularly as those approaches are not synonymous. Debate among analysts and political groups will be particularly sharp concerning continued employment of Palestinians within Israel during the interim period and also over the direction of future external trade.

During the negotiating period the PLO and OT Palestinians could work to prepare development plans for the interim stage, ameliorate relations in the region, and deepen contact with foreign aid donors and lenders. The PLO's Central Council called on 23 April 1991 for enhanced efforts to build the Palestinian national economy by preparing development plans in all sectors and coordinating the multiple levels and forms of institutions in the OT. Moreover, the PLO's Economic Department is drafting plans for the regulating of and investment in a market economy during the transition phase, based in part on providing legal guarantees to the private sector and also on the formation of a development bank, supported by Palestinian businessmen in the diaspora.[32] Projects that are developed primarily in Tunis risk being inappropriate for OT needs and therefore careful consideration of OT priorities and continual interaction between internal and external planners will be essential, if those plans are to bear fruit.

Coordinated fund-raising, channeling of aid and securing investment would be vital at a time of reduced Arab donations; this could be achieved through a strengthened Palestine National Fund and enhanced planning and economic coordinating activities.[33] The PLO already discusses priorities and programs in the OT with representatives of the European Community. That model, by which the EC meets separately with the PLO and with a Palestinian committee in the OT, could be utilized by other foreign donors. PLO efforts would also encompass Palestinian communities in Lebanon and Jordan, and deal with the special problem of assisting the Palestinians expelled from Kuwait. Coordinated efforts with key Arab countries concerning fundraising, investing, water resource planning, and opening Arab markets for exports from the OT would benefit the Palestinian communities and help to reduce inter-Arab tension. The PLO would need to stress reopening Arab markets for OT exports and convince Jordan to end its boycott of manufactured goods from the OT.

International Agencies

International actors already endorse the application of the Fourth Geneva Convention to the OT and therefore should work, during the negotiations, to encourage Israel to implement its provisions as well as to carry out confidence-building measures. Bilateral negotiations with the Israeli government on economic aid and trade could stress the importance of Israel's adopting measures to ease economic hardships in the OT and to reduce restrictions on the OT economy.

International aid agencies' programs would be directed toward enhancing the economic viability of the OT and would seek to support and enlarge indigenous resources.[34] (This issue is discussed at length in relation to the interim period, see pp. 140-142.) The agencies would work with those indigenous institutions, which would play key roles in determining priorities and would help design and control the specific projects. A shift might begin from direct grants for technical assistance and loans that could be sustained by local resources and expertise. Direct grants would be limited to the infrastructure and to pilot projects that would be financially risky for local investors or that need a one-time infusion of capital funds. Foreign development agencies would emphasize helping Palestinians to establish the knowledge-base and skills essential to implement economic programs during the transitional and subsequent stages. Some agencies already adopt these approaches, but a more comprehensive effort could be made, particularly in relation to:

- **Market surveys:** Support product-specific, in-depth market surveys by Palestinians in order to develop a sound basis for deciding what new products should be introduced, what existing areas should be expanded, altered or contracted, and how marketing of produce and products could be improved locally and for export; include funds to publish and disseminate the findings widely to Palestinian businesses.[35]

- **Infrastructure studies:** Fund and provide technical assistance for long-range analyses of infrastructure needs as well as specific feasibility studies, including road systems, housing estates, electricity requirements, and communications networks.[36]

- **Skills development:** Provide technical assistance in areas in which limited skills exist currently in the OT, such as quality control programs for food and drugs and analyses of environmental pollution.

- **Management training:** Underwrite training and educational programs to enhance indigenous technical and management skills, including support for the establishment of new polytechnic institutes in the OT.

- **Credit planning:** Survey the credit needs of each sector in order to plan a rational allocation of funds as credit institutions are established and expanded during the interim period. Medium level institutions, which can handle $50,000 to $500,000 loans, are particularly needed and require external financial and technical support.[37]

- **Standardization and consumer education:** Support the efforts of Palestinian institutions to foster standardized production standards in industry and agriculture and to educate consumers about such standards. Training programs could be supported in pharmacies, factories, and hospitals, for staff working in laboratories and handling patient records. Agricultural extension programs could be fostered with farmers concerning pesticides, chemical fertilizers and water quality.

Israeli Interest in Economic Improvements and Potential Trade

Arab governments would offer valuable inducements to Israel to negotiate by addressing, in regional negotiations, specific possibilities for trade and the joint development of resources. Those benefits would be contingent upon the outcome of negotiations for Palestinian self-rule and for peace with Syria, Lebanon and Jordan. Four measures might involve:

- **Lifting restrictions:** Jordan's lifting its ban on importing goods from the OT that have Israeli components.

- **Oil:** Initiation of discussions by Gulf Cooperation Council (GCC) negotiators with Israel on the terms and arrangements for oil sales in the event of peace.

- **Joint market planning:** Establishment of a joint committee to outline plans for future economic relations, with Israeli and Arab experts, businessmen, industrialists and farmers, in order to enhance Israeli interest in attaining peace accords through which they would gain access to Arab markets.

- **Water resource master plan:** Initiation of multilateral planning for regional water resource use, incorporating various options and comprehensiveness of design. (This issue is detailed in the section on the interim period.)[38]

Such actions taken during the negotiating period by the Arab states would serve as confidence-building measures for Israel, reducing Israeli concerns about implacable Arab hostility and fostering changes in the perceptions, attitudes and partisan preferences of the Israeli public. The process of drafting plans for regional water use would be particularly useful, since many Israelis see water scarcity as a key obstacle to peace. Planning would indicate that cooperative approaches are feasible and that the conflict need not remain zero-sum. Moreover, the prospect of peace accords might well attract further investment to Israel itself which would assist the process of absorbing Soviet and other Jews, since investors have been deterred by the climate of political and economic instability.[39]

The negotiating process would enhance the leverage of those Israelis who support moves to bolster the OT economy and to resolve the political conflict with the Arab world. Nonetheless, motivations would be mixed: some would see a positive value in helping Palestinians become economically self-reliant in anticipation of disengaging politically from Israel; some would perceive a gain for Israeli security if fewer Palestinians worked inside Israel and economic distress were alleviated; and others would believe that reducing the cost of controlling the OT would ease Israel's absorption of Soviet Jews and other immigrants. The government would perceive moves to strengthen the OT economy in the context of instituting limited self-rule.[40]

Israel would also anticipate long-term benefits through Palestinian entrepreneurs who might help to open the door to the Arab world for Israeli commerce. Current joint research by Israeli and Palestinian economists, while focused primarily on scenarios for economic development in the OT itself, also address the issues of the impact of peace on the Israeli economy and the implications of a regional economic union, embracing Israel, the OT and Jordan.[41] A limited number of Palestinians and Israelis would seize the opportunity created by negotiations to initiate discussion of joint economic projects, in which jobs and profits would benefit both parties. Those could range across industry, agriculture, energy, transportation and tourism. Israelis would perceive a long-term potential in such business relations, since a peace accord would open up markets in the Arab world for those goods. Such positive inducements by Palestinian entrepreneurs and Arab regimes could have the effect of shifting the balance within Israel, since the anticipated benefits would be contingent on empowering Palestinians. Nonetheless, during the period of negotiations, those positive incentives would remain limited and hypothetical, not yet realizable given the insecure political climate.

The Interim Period

A dynamic and stable economy in the OT is a *sine qua non* for the success of an interim self-government. During the period of Palestinian self-rule, substantial change would occur in the economy with the introduction of Palestinian-led economic planning, removal or reduction in trade barriers, and expansion of sources of credit and employment. A meaningful interim self-governing authority (ISGA) would need to have policymaking authority, administrative control and coordinating functions. Israeli businesses would begin to trade with Arab countries as the first step in a new interaction between the Israeli and Arab economic sectors; in addition, regional resource planning would accelerate.

Removal of Barriers

In order to stabilize economic life during the interim period, substantial efforts would be needed to remove barriers in all economic areas, particularly in monetary, foreign exchange and foreign trade policies. That would not only meet immediate needs of the

ISGA but would lay the foundation for viable economic activity and future development. Such steps would include:

• **Trade barriers:** Barriers to the movement of goods among Israel, the OT and Jordan would be gradually reduced along with restrictions on trade between businesses in the OT and abroad. A joint committee would coordinate trade, ensuring adherence to quality, health and labeling standards and serving as an appeals board.

• **Restrictions on credit and capital-imports facilities:** Banks that previously operated in the OT would reopen or new ones might be established, with abnormal restrictions on deposits lifted and provision made for commercial, industrial, mortgage and agricultural loans.[42] Banks would adhere to the overall regulations of the Bank of Israel. They would be allowed to use both Israeli currency and foreign hard currencies. Individuals and agencies outside the OT would be allowed to open accounts and deposit funds in the banks.

• **Barriers to population movement:** Restrictions on the movement of Palestinians into Israel for visits or work would be lifted and workers would be able to reside temporarily in Israel, rather than commute daily. Such movement would be subject only to security considerations, agreed upon between the ISGA and the Israeli government. Palestinian workers would be registered and subject to Israeli labor laws, insurance benefits and taxes, the latter being transferred to the OT for use by the ISGA's social service offices.

Labor Mobility

The issue of the labor market is critical to the OT economy and in this case the ISGA may face a dilemma. On the one hand, if the flow of labor to Israel ceases, the large, sudden addition to the OT's domestic labor supply would cause a drastic drop in wages and would exacerbate unemployment. An abrupt shift might also induce emigration from the OT, although that would depend partly on the availability of jobs in Jordan and the Gulf. On the other hand, leaving the labor market open also has its drawbacks since it would generate competition for workers with the Israeli market, which pays higher wages than OT employers. Nonetheless, if accompanied by lifting barriers to trade and investment, the Palestinian domestic base would grow and the downward pressure on the labor market

121

would be relatively moderate. On balance, therefore, the ISGA is apt to decide to leave the borders open to labor commuting and let the domestic product grow gradually.[43]

The ISGA will have to take into account the probable political weight of Palestinian trade unions in the transitional period. Released from years of repression and semi-clandestine existence, they will seek to incorporate as many workers as possible into their ranks, to provide health, educational and social services for members, and to flex their muscles in wage and benefit negotiations with Palestinian employers.[44] They may also want a role in regulating labor flow to Israel, through labor exchanges that would register workers and monitor the wages, benefits and standards at the job site. The General Federation of Trade Unions (GFTU) would seek to bargain with Israeli employers on behalf of Palestinian workers and to handle the disbursal of Histadrut benefits that would accrue to those workers. Those benefits could underwrite unemployment benefits, training and assistance for handicapped and disabled workers, health services, and a capital fund for credit for small businesses. The GFTU would thereby influence the policies of the ISGA, particularly in relation to unemployment and welfare benefits. The over-supply of labor in the OT might limit the unions' success in contract negotiations; but their political impact is potentially high.

Financial and Monetary Authority

The ISGA would have independent sources of finance and mechanisms to enforce its decisions. New structures would be established on a phased basis, including a central bureau of statistics, a trade board with the power to issue licenses, a bureau of standards, a bureau of vehicles, population and land registration offices, and an agricultural extension service. A labor board would supervise labor exchanges that would regularize contract labor in Israel and coordinate the movement of labor to Arab countries. ISGA systems for social security, education, training, and health would be formed. Regional and urban planning offices would begin to assess the long-term structural needs of the OT.

The ISGA's financial powers will need to include the right to levy taxes, e.g., income, VAT and/or sales, and the right to negotiate and receive grants and loans from abroad. The ISGA would receive the OT's share of tax, tariff, and social security payments. It might also negotiate with Israel for backpayment of taxes and worker funds collected from OT residents since June 1967 that were used by Israel outside the OT. Initially, taxes, tariffs, and fees would need to remain proportionately at the same level as Israel's, assuming that open trade relations are instituted. A joint committee, however, could review specific items so that specific changes might be instituted by the end of the interim period.

In terms of economic policy, interim arrangements would be judged by the yardstick of their impact on the long-term objective of full independence for Palestinians in making economic decisions.[45] Nonetheless, to the extent that free mobility for goods and labor is preserved, coordination is necessary concerning monetary policy and foreign exchange management as well as taxes and tariffs. Two different price-sets or currencies are impossible where there are no barriers to movement. In the interim period, Israeli currency would continue to circulate in the OT, and the ISGA would not be able to establish a separate central bank. Klinov suggests that OT delegates be represented in Israeli decision-making bodies as an interim measure, to ensure that their needs were met. However, Palestinians might prefer the formation of a new Israeli-Palestinian coordinating body, which would not merge Palestinian institutions into the existing Israeli framework. That joint body could arrange, for example, the payment to the ISGA of its share of tariffs collected at Israeli entry points.[46] The coordinating body could also help to cushion the potential impact of inflation on the OT economy by arranging for the Israeli Central Bank to allocate to the OT the extra income collected from OT residents.

Economic Planning

The ISGA would give serious and sustained attention to economic planning, including assessing which sectors would be accorded priority for economic expansion.[47] The planning department will be a critically important component of the ISGA bureaucracy, but it would not be empowered to micromanage projects.

Immediate improvements could take place in areas under municipal and village authority. They could rehabilitate long-neglected schools, clinics, roads, electricity systems, and water supplies. A regulated system for raising funds through bonds, taxes and fees would need to be instituted.

Palestinian planners would also see infrastructural development as a means to reduce dependence on employment in Israel. The construction of housing projects for refugees currently in OT camps, for example, could absorb labor and utilize the skills of architects, engineers, electricians, and plumbers. The hope is to build 100,000 houses on the eastern highlands of the West Bank (20,000 units yearly) for 600,000 refugees who now live in substandard housing in camps in the OT, and to construct 5000 kilometers of roads, particularly linking the north and south of the West Bank and replacing inadequate village roads. These projects would simultaneously serve political, social and economic functions.

More ambitious projects might await resolution of the OT's final status. Nonetheless, the ISGA planning apparatus would investigate long-range development options, including the implications of absorbing Palestinians now living in Arab countries. A key difficulty that the ISGA will face is that important sources of human and physical capital lie outside the OT. Skilled labor, professionals and management personnel are available in abundance in the Palestinian diaspora.[48] Since only a limited number of Palestinians will be able to return to the OT during the interim period, a system would need to be devised to channel Palestinian expertise and funds to viable projects. Palestinian diaspora willingness to invest substantially in the OT would also depend on knowing whether the interim period would lead to a satisfactory final status. While residents of the OT would risk investing during the interim period, Palestinians abroad would be inhibited by the still-uncertain political climate.

Agriculture

The expansion of agriculture will be limited, in part, by the scarcity of water resources in the OT (see section below). Nonetheless, in the context of a fair share of water being allocated to the OT and land in the Jordan Valley being restored to Palestinian farmers, a considerable increase in irrigated agriculture is possible in the West Bank. Fishing can be expanded in the Gaza Strip and aquaculture introduced, using off-shore cages and feeding the fish garbage and algae. Agricultural productivity can be enhanced by expanding the use of drip irrigation and plastic greenhouses, by using crops and fruits that require limited or brackish water, and by investing in waste water for irrigation. Agricultural marketing could be improved by up-grading the municipal wholesale markets, doubling the capacity of refrigerated storage warehouses, reconstituting grain silos, and constructing specialized centers to prepare produce for export. Computerized information systems would provide up-to-date data on local and foreign demand, quality inspectors would insure standards, and agricultural extension agents would advise farmers on the latest techniques.[49]

On the West Bank highlands, the ISGA would need to tackle the problem of desertification, caused by overgrazing as the area available for pasture has been severely limited. Former pasture land would need to be restored and afforestation resumed. The ISGA would need access to satellite and remote sensing data and information from weather stations in order to assess rates of evaporation and precipitation, study soils and plants, and monitor weather patterns. Moreover, comprehensive studies of environmental pollution caused by pesticides, herbicides, human waste, and industrial refuse would be vital. Those studies would form the basis for systematic efforts to educate farmers concerning proper use of chemicals, to expand the network of piped water, and to regulate industries' disposal of waste.

Key Industries to Expand

Industrial development is currently even more limited than agriculture, and requires not only a relatively predictable political climate but also a substantial investment in capital and skills training. There is only limited capital available among residents and the territory has lost skilled personnel.[50] Nonetheless, Palestinians are interested in investing; they require institutions that they can trust and a sense that regulations will not change abruptly and arbitrarily.

Given those limitations, the ISGA would encourage economic projects that would capitalize on existing skills and benefit from the OT's comparative advantages. ISGA guidelines that minimize government regulation would enable small businesses and industries to flourish, according to international economists Patrick Clawson and Howard Rosen. Their sales to Israel would benefit the Palestinians, while remaining too small to dislocate the Israeli economy.[51] Market surveys and technical feasibility studies will be essential before investors expand their operations. Areas that would be potentially productive during the interim period include:

- **Pharmaceuticals and cosmetics:** A strong base already exists, with Palestinian companies controlling two-thirds of the West Bank market; with mandatory quality controls, enhanced research, and aggressive marketing in Israel and the Arab world, they could become competitive and profitable.

- **Clothing and textiles:** Given the strong skill-base among residents of the OT in textiles and clothing manufacture, the main requirement would be a shift from sub-contracting to Palestinian-owned businesses. Despite potential competition from cheaper Egyptian and Syrian clothing, Palestinian sales in the Arab world could fill specialty niches.

- **Shoemaking:** OT cobblers and small-scale shoe factories produce shoes that could compete in Israel, using local tanned skins. Shoemaking could expand with additional capital, quality control and access to foreign markets.

- **Light industries:** Potential expansion in plastic products, household kitchenware, toiletry articles, furniture, and crafts for tourists is considerable, given the level of existing skills and the relatively low level of capitalization required. Management and marketing would need improvement, and such production would be primarily consumed locally.

- **Agricultural industries:** The production of canned fruits and vegetables, bottled juices, baked goods, biscuits, milled flour and processed dairy products could be expanded markedly once restrictions are lifted and fair competition instituted. Fodder factories and plants to make cartons, metal cans, glass bottles, and plastic containers would also be constructed.[52] Local capital seeks to expand those industries, which would rely on local raw materials and relatively unskilled labor.

- **Fishing industries:** The Gaza Strip would serve as the center for fish packing, freezing and canning factories, based on local resources and labor.

- **Agricultural technology:** Poultry hatcheries, feed plants, cow-breeding stations and tissue culture for dates would be established rapidly to meet the needs of OT farmers. Foreign development agencies are eager to assist Palestinian agricultural cooperatives in introducing those technologies.

- **Quarrying:** The stone quarries on the West Bank are a prime source of construction materials in the OT and Jordan, but require up-dating in operations and marketing.[53] Exports would expand once restrictions were lifted on transit beyond Jordan to the Arab world.

Utilization of Land Resources

The issue of control over land resources would be particularly important. Palestinians critical of the negotiating process emphasize their fear that self-rule will exclude those resources.[54] For meaningful self-rule, either the ISGA would control land during the interim period or a joint Israeli-Palestinian body would determine land use. Purchase and seizure of land by Israel would cease and construction of settlements would halt. A Palestinian land registry department would be established. Municipal and regional zoning boards would develop new plans for the coordinated use of land for residential, industrial and agricultural purposes.

Residents would need access to what is now identified as public land and absentee land, as well as much of the land that has been closed for military purposes. Land registration would resume. Since some estimate that only 8-9 percent of the West Bank land is used by settlements, Palestinians could gain the use of considerable tracts without affecting the settlements. *Miri* and *mawat* land could revert to Palestinian control. The most tangible impact would be in irrigated areas of the Jordan valley and grazing land on the eastern slopes of the highlands.

Barring the Israeli government and citizens from confiscating land and other property during the interim period could reduce the chilling effect on investment and lending caused by Palestinian fears of collateralizing their property and could stimulate the financial sector significantly, by freeing up huge amounts of currently unused collateral.

Since it cannot be expected that the Israeli government would accord full authority over land to the interim Palestinian institutions, a joint body is the most realistic alternative. Such a joint commission would assess current land use and also examine the status of settlements, which have been built on varying categories of land. In the case of settlements a value would be placed on the assets (houses, schools, clinics, etc.) of the settlements, with the expectation that Israel would receive financial compensation if it turned over their assets intact to the ISGA at the end of the interim phase. The body would also examine land-expropriation records to establish what compensation and payments would be due to Palestinians whose land had been seized and altered during the Israeli occupation. The Israeli government would form a separate body to decide on the method of reintegrating settlers into Israel. And the Palestinian authority would establish a separate procedure for compensating the original landowners for land that the authority would need to retain for public purposes, including the settlement of refugees and returnees.

Electricity

Use and control over electricity could be initially contentious, and so a joint board might be established to sort out disagreements. During the course of the occupation Israel has linked the OT electricity system into the Israeli grid, sometimes by preventing Palestinian towns and villages from installing or replacing their own electricity generators. However, under the interim phase, control of electricity would not be crucial to Israel and therefore the ISGA might assume authority without undue difficulty. Clawson and Rosen suggest that the Palestinian consumers should be left to decide whether they want to keep the links to the Israeli electricity system or establish a separate (and probably more costly) network under the ISGA. They comment that it is "naive to think that compelling Palestinians to depend upon Israeli electricity" will dampen their desire for independence.[55] Nonetheless, measures would have to be agreed upon during the interim period for the guaranteed supply of a specified level of electricity at agreed upon rates, so that the ISGA population would not be hostage to arbitrary or politically-motivated supply cuts or rate increases.

Alternatively, the Jerusalem Electricity Company could purchase electricity from Jordan, since its plant at Awja is only a few miles from the East Bank. Establishing an independent electricity system during the interim period would probably not be economical. However, plans might be made to generate electricity as part of the potential desalinization plant in Gaza (see below).

Local Water Development

Water use would be based on the principles of mutual respect and equitable distribution. Israeli experts tend to agree with Palestinian experts that Israelis and Palestinians should be entitled to an equal allocation of fresh water per person for domestic use, with industrial and agricultural use based on a fair market price. Hillel Shuval, for example, proposes that 100 cubic meters per person per year would provide a hygienic standard for urban life and industrial development. Substantial water conservation, waste water recycling, and a restructuring of agriculture would be necessary to meet those needs; even so, Shuval argues, imported water would be required by Israel and the OT within a decade.[56]

Comprehensive planning concerning water and related environmental issues would be top priority for the ISGA. Israeli experts indicate that water plants and master plans require at least fifteen years to design and construct, and therefore systematic attention must be given to water issues early in the interim period. In the short run, agreements would be signed with the Israeli water authorities for the guaranteed supply of water through existing pipelines so that the public would not be hostage to political shifts in Israel. Planning and enforcement of standards in relation to environmental pollution will be required, including analyses of the polluting of ground water by fertilizers, pesticides, and garbage disposal by towns, villages and Israeli settlements. Particular water management issues include (see Figure 5, p. 130):

- **Access to ground water from the West Bank and Gaza aquifers:** Joint Israeli-Palestinian monitoring of the use, level and quality of the aquifers will be essential for restructuring the use of water in Israel and the OT and ensuring that neither party can deprive the other of vital water supplies. Regulations concerning Palestinian wells would be altered to balance the need for enhanced water resources with the danger from overpumping; Israel would institute water-saving measures (particularly in settlements in the OT) and prevent its deep-bore wells from drying up Palestinian wells in the West Bank or depleting the Gaza aquifer; and joint planning would begin for the long-term rehabilitation of aquifers.

- **Access to the eastern aquifer:** Palestinians could gain immediate access to and control over pumping from the eastern aquifer that drains toward the Jordan River, since that has no link to the Israeli hydrologic cycle and flows entirely within the West Bank.[57] Planning would be undertaken to construct dams on the four major *wadis* (seasonal rivers) on the eastern slope.[58]

- **Waste water for irrigation:** Israeli hydrologists estimate that half of the fresh water used in households in the OT could be recycled through waste water plants and sedimentation ponds.[59] Those estimates might prove high; moreover, preliminary studies indicate that recycling is costly. However, recycled water would help meet agricultural needs in localities on the central West Bank and would ease the shortage in Gaza, particularly when

Figure 5
Principal Aquifers Serving Israel and the West Bank

Source: Hillel Shuval, "Approaches to Finding an Equitable Solution to the Water Resources Problems Shared by Israel and the Palestinians Over the Use of Mountain Aquifers," p. 28. In *Water: Conflict or Cooperation*, Gershon Baskin (Jerusalem: IPCRI, I:2, May 1992).

accompanied by shifts in crops, fruits and methods of cultivation. Initially high costs of constructing the projects might be met by external funding, but farmers would pay a market price for the water.

- **Water storage projects:** Replenishing of the Gaza and West Bank aquifers could be enhanced by the relatively low-cost construction of small dams on *wadis* (seasonal rivers and streams) and by the high-cost construction of storm water preservation systems in cities. The latter, which require external funding, is already underway in Gaza City in a project to channel rain water through underground pipes into an artificial lake which will help to recharge the water table and irrigate nearby groves as well as eliminate urban traffic and health hazards.[60]

- **Desalinization in Gaza:** Two types of desalinization are proposed by Palestinian experts: a relatively inexpensive project to convert brackish water into drinkable water by reverse osmosis and a costly project to distill sea water and generate electricity.[61] Israeli experts have proposed a joint plant, on the border between Gaza and Israel, that would also supply parts of the Negev and the southern West Bank. Despite the high capital investment and on-going fuel costs, some experts argue that consumers, greenhouse-agriculture and certain industries could afford the water.

Restructuring the use of ground water on an equitable basis would thus be supplemented by local sewage and desalinization projects that would meet local needs during the interim period. Regional water projects, however, would be valuable as means to share the available water on a more comprehensive basis. They would also enhance the storage of water and thereby increase the water available to the countries.

Regional Water Projects

At present, there are severe imbalances in the availability of water among Middle Eastern countries. Israel and Jordan, for example, each use 108 percent of their safe-use stocks, which degrades their water stocks and depletes their aquifers and rivers. The declining water stock in the Jordan River basin raises the level of tension among the riparians, water-expert Thomas Naff argues.[62] Israel's control over the Hazbani headwaters of the Jordan River, located on the Golan Heights, is also subject to negotiations with

Syria. Turkey and Lebanon, in contrast, have ample water supplies. If Israel controlled the entire Litani River in Lebanon, its water supply would increase by 50 percent. However, forcible seizure of that vital resource would create more strategic problems than it would resolve. The government apparently anticipates that negotiations with Lebanon will enable it to purchase a substantial amount of water from the Litani and Awali in return for withdrawing from the "security zone" in the south. Turkey has proposed constructing a "peace" pipeline through Syria that would ease the shortages in Jordan and Israel, but that proposal has political and logistical complications. Experts argue that longterm solutions will come not only from restructuring regional economies in order to economize on water but also from comprehensive regional water-supply plans, including new storage facilities, desalinization, and systems to recycle waste water.

Israel would view the establishment of regional resource plans as a positive incentive to reducing its own control over water in the OT. The water issue would become less critical and Israel could show greater flexibility along the lines noted earlier. The five options sketched here would each require an extended period of time for implementation, and thus would affect the long-term status as well as the interim period:

- **Jordan River:** Completing Jordan's Unity Dam would store the flood waters of the Yarmouk River, which flows into the Jordan River, and provide vital domestic, industrial and agricultural water for Jordan. Syria has already been promised most of the hydroelectric power to be generated and would continue to use water from the Yarmouk. Israel could gain hydroelectric power and regularize its access to Yarmouk water. The West Ghor canal could be constructed in the West Bank, as anticipated prior to 1967. The Unity Dam would reduce pressure on Israel to release fresh water stored in Lake Tiberias (Sea of Galilee) for use by downstream Jordanian and Palestinian agriculture.[63]

- **Desalination:** A joint Israeli-Jordanian plant for Eilat and Aqaba could meet common water needs in those growing port cities. Since energy costs are the main expense in desalinization, once the plant has been constructed, the cheapest desalinated water would be produced in the Gulf states where gas is often flared rather than utilized. The water could then be piped north to Jordan/Palestine and Israel for domestic use.[64]

- **Litani River:** A multilateral study of the utilization of water from the Litani River in Lebanon and its potential for meeting regional demand for domestic water and hydroelectric power could pave the way to long-term accords among Lebanon, Syria, Jordan, Palestine and Israel for its shared use. Lebanon would sell the water on a commercial basis. In the past, Israeli experts have proposed that such water be piped to and stored in Lake Tiberias. However, recognizing the political sensitivity of that proposal, some Israelis now suggest that part of the water be stored behind Unity Dam, with joint inspection and management. Increasing demand and development in Lebanon itself, however, would limit the availability of such water to, perhaps, forty years.[66]

- **Turkish pipeline:** The transport of water for 600 kilometers from rivers in south-west Turkey through Syria and Jordan to the West Bank would entail high initial capital costs. Its operating cost could be higher than piped water from the Litani but potentially less expensive than desalinization.[66] Nonetheless, such a massive multi-country pipeline would pose political and logistical problems and require a form of joint management. (The example of oil pipelines that cross multiple national borders indicates that accords are possible but that access can be severed in the event of political or military strife.) Israeli and Palestinian experts tend to agree that investing in efficient energy, waste water systems and desalinization would be preferable, at this time, to relying on a long distance pipeline from Turkey.

- **Nile pipeline:** Israeli experts propose a pipeline to bring emergency supplies of water from the Nile to the Gaza Strip, based on extending the existing pipeline from el-Arish to Rafah.[67] The water would be purchased at commercial rates on the basis of a forty year contract. Subsequently, Egypt would lack any excess water and reduced desalinization costs might make that a feasible alternative for Gaza. Egypt, however, is wary of exporting Nile water and Palestinians prefer alternatives based on local water sources or desalinization. Although the water from the pipeline would be a third of the current cost of desalinated water, this project is unlikely to be realized.

Israeli Trade with the Arab World

During the interim period, Israel would begin to gain commercial benefits from trade with the Arab world. A limited number of private Israeli-Palestinian joint ventures would be launched in the OT, largely geared toward trade in the Middle East. GCC oil might begin to flow to Israel, by a pipeline across Jordan or by tanker to Eilat. Official consultative committees, linking Israel and the relevant Arab states, would expand their discussion of trade to develop a strategy for maximizing economic relations under conditions of Israeli withdrawal from the occupied territories and peace between Israel and its Arab neighbors. By formalizing contact with individuals from Arab countries, the meetings would lead toward normalized relations. The committees' findings would provide concrete information about the benefits of peace and might increase Israeli willingness to compromise in order to obtain these benefits. The committees would provide a framework for bargaining over non-ideological issues where a mutually beneficial outcome is possible, and hence contribute to building confidence and momentum.

External Agencies' Roles

The United States government, European Community, Japan and such international agencies as the International Monetary Fund, World Bank and UN Development Program would play useful roles in supporting the economic restructuring adopted by Israel and the ISGA during the interim period. International assistance given directly to the ISGA would bolster its authority and help it undertake difficult planning and development programs. Assistance to regional programs in which Israel and Arab governments participate would increase their incentives to cooperate in long-term resource development. Free trade and/or preferential trade agreements between the ISGA and Washington and the EC would encourage domestic production for export. Comparable agreements with Israel could be linked to concrete steps by the Israeli government to grant financial and economic authority to the ISGA and to share with the ISGA authority over the allocation of water, electricity and land resources.

The Palestinian assets not only include human resources, noted earlier, but also somewhat paradoxical administrative assets. One development specialist noted that the ISGA has the advantage of not inheriting an overdeveloped bureaucracy, an entrenched system of public subsidies, or a public debt, unlike most less developed countries. International programs might thereby avoid the mistakes made in other developing countries, if they structure their assistance appropriately. In relations with donors, moreover, the indigenous groups and institutions should be clearly in charge of setting priorities, designing and channelling economic aid and social assistance. Aid programs must be structured in such a fashion as to be compatible with future moves toward independence and to help the economy and social institutions prepare for a sustainable independence when it is achieved. Forms of assistance during the interim period — which would also apply in the final status — would include:

• **Direct grants:** Grants would be limited to three types —

(1) **large-scale infrastructure projects** such as waste water schemes and the desalinization plant in Gaza, for which the price of water produced could not be expected to cover the capital cost of the initial construction. Village and municipal infrastructure projects could also be supported by grants, given their limited resources;

(2) **one-time start-up capital or pilot projects** for local industries whose infrastructure or planning needs exceed indigenous financial resources but which would be particularly valuable to the OT economy. Otherwise, grants for private limited- interest projects should be avoided; and, (3) **a "safety net"** in the form of food and social aid for groups facing particular hardships during the period of adjustment to self-rule. All projects would be implemented by Palestinian organizations, with the foreign donor providing only the technical advice that they seek.

• **Loans and investments:** Loans should be channelled through indigenous credit institutions, by providing them with capital and management advice, in preference to foreign agencies making loans directly to individual businesses, factories or farms. Housing loans and the establishment of mortgage agencies will be particularly important, given the anticipated emphasis on that sector. External agencies can help to ensure that loans are directed to those enterprises and activities that have the potential to flourish in an increasingly independent economy. They could also try to assure that import-export restrictions would not strangle the new enterprises. Those considerations would become part of the donors' political interactions with both Israel and the Palestinian community.

• **Technical Assistance:** Where technical skills are not available within the OT, such as in large-scale water and land reclamation

135

projects and specialized high technology fields, international agencies could provide expert advice and personnel to assist the ISGA in planning and implementing infrastructure programs.

- **Training and Education:** Training components are essential parts of assistance programs and can often be implemented in conjunction with local universities, schools and business enterprises. Management and administrative training for Palestinian PVOs would strengthen their organizational capacity.[68] Aid agencies could enhance polytechnic, agricultural and business programs in the OT in order to help develop the skills essential to the future independent nation. Teacher-training at the elementary and secondary levels could also be fostered. Palestinians should establish priorities for their educational needs, through such a body as the Council for Higher Education and the ISGA planning office, and ensure coordination in training among foreign agencies.

- **Regional Programs:** International technical and financial assistance could prove vital to resolving regional resource issues, notably the construction of Unity Dam; the transfer of appropriate technologies and training and research so Israeli and Arab scientists and technicians can tackle water-related problems; planning the restructuring of their economies; and providing a financial cushion against serious economic and social dislocations.[69] Such multidimensional programs would assist the regional states in establishing viable programs and mutually beneficial relationships that would help to sustain the peace accords.

Such carefully calibrated involvement by external agencies in assisting Palestinian social and economic institutions would provide valuable support for the interim period. The limited patterns of aid that have existed during the occupation would be reformulated within the context of the increasing independence of the Palestinian society and the restructuring of its economy.

The Long Term Status

For both Israel and the Palestinians the quality of long term economic interactions will to a significant degree depend upon the quality of economic relationships enjoyed during the interim period. The Palestinian institutions that were established during the in-terim phase would become fully functioning by the final phase. Their precise characteristics would depend on the form of the link of the Palestinian sovereign authority (PSA) with Jordan; in an independent state, Jordan and Palestine would not formally integrate their financial and economic institutions, whereas varying degrees of linkage and integration would be established in a loose confederation, partially centralized federation, or completely unified political system. Nonetheless, even if Jordan and Palestine were politically separate, an economic union or Benelux type free trade zone might be established. Such a zone could include Israel and would require coordinating institutions to handle complex issues of currencies, tariffs, subsidies, and labor movement. Existing models and experiments in Europe can provide important examples of success and failure. The approaches noted below are offered as examples of steps that might be taken by a Palestinian governing authority. Choices will, of course, be made by the local population and its government.

Resources and Infrastructure

Basic issues involving resources would be finalized at this stage, including permanent arrangements for the control and use of electricity and water in the OT and for the control of air, water, and land pollution. The joint and regional bodies established during the interim period would be transformed into permanent institutions whose powers would be codified internationally and written into the several bilateral peace treaties. Specific aspects include:

- **Housing, Industrial Zones and Roads:** Full-scale development of the infrastructure of the PSA area might include expanding electricity, water and communication systems in order to meet housing, agricultural and industrial needs. Industrial zones might be established adjacent to the major towns and housing projects for refugees and returnees would be constructed on the mountain ridges of the West Bank and in the Gaza Strip. An integrated economic plan might be implemented in the Jordan Valley, based on high-tech agriculture. The construction of north-south roads on the West Bank would be completed. International aid would be needed if Israel and the PSA agree to construct a highway connecting the West Bank and the Gaza Strip. (Alternatively, Japan or the EC could build a high-speed monorail connecting the two regions.)

- **Gaza port:** The port would be totally overhauled in order to handle international cargo, including refrigerated ships for agricultural produce and container ships for industrial exports. A free trade and industrial zone might be established in conjunction with the Gaza port. Palestinian experts indicate that investments in commerce and the basic infrastructure are higher priority in the interim period than reconstructing the port, since they anticipate making arrangements to ship through Israeli ports; however, in the long-run they would probably want their own seaport.[70]

- **Airports:** The small airport at Qalandiya, northern Jerusalem, would be expanded and upgraded to serve as an international airport, handling cargo trade and tourism. A small airport might be built in Gaza at a later stage, for local and regional use.[71]

- **Land Use:** Land and settlement issues would be finalized according to a jointly articulated plan, including the transfer of the assets and land of settlements to the PSA and the phased relocation of most Israeli settlers, with international financial assistance to Israel. Individual Israelis who purchased land in the OT from Palestinians would have special compensation if they choose to leave.[72] Land restored to Palestinian authority would be initially controlled by the PSA, for public use and for settling returnees, some of whom might be housed in former Israeli settlements. The PSA would have to compensate Palestinians whose land could not be returned to them since it was required for public use.

- **Local Water Use:** Joint Israeli-Palestinian planning during the interim period would have led to a substantial revision in the shares of ground water resources originating in the OT and Israel so that residents would have relatively equal access to water for basic needs. Palestinians would thus gain increased access to fresh drinking water. Their municipalities and village councils would emphasize the establishment and maintenance of piped water systems and the PSA would focus on completing projects to recycle waste water, store rain water and desalinate brackish and sea water in Gaza. The joint Israeli-Palestinian body would continue to monitor the level of water use in Israel and the PSA to ensure compliance, assisted by remote sensing devices.

- **Regional Water and Electricity:** The Unity Dam would be completed by the end of the interim period, enabling Jordan, Syria and Israel to increase their water and electricity supplies.

Construction might also have begun on water storage and hydroelectric power plants on the Litani River, with plans outlined for the sale of water and electricity to Syria, Jordan/Palestine and Israel and provisional arrangements made for the storage of excess water in Lake Tiberias and behind Unity Dam. Construction would have begun for a desalinization plant linking Eilat and Aqaba. The potential pipelines from Turkey or Egypt would have been costed, and their political complications assessed. Costing as well as environmental implications of nuclear plants to desalinate water might also be explored. Jordan and Israel would have embarked on major reforms in their water-use programs, in order to economize on that scarce resource. Given the centrality of water to the lives of all the riparians in the Jordan basin, ongoing multilateral systems for consultation, research and coordination would be essential in cooperation with international development agencies.[73]

Long-Term Development

A full discussion of the possible characteristics of the Palestinian economy in the final phase lies beyond the scope of this study. However, certain areas can be highlighted, which would build on indigenous skills and incorporate the expertise of Palestinians who might return from the diaspora. The project-areas outlined for the transitional phase would continue to be developed. Planning and investment would begin in all these areas during the interim period, in anticipation of their full fruition later on.

- **Construction:** Palestinians are skilled in all aspects of construction from architect and engineer to plasterer, electrician, tile layer and plumber. Those skills would be honed during the interim period. Once the major demand for housing and industrial construction among residents and returnees is met, the construction trades could serve as the basis for export-oriented services and industries in the neighboring countries.

- **Tourism:** Palestinian skills in tourism would be developed and consolidated to provide summer resorts for Arabs in the mild climate of the hilly areas, to expand winter tourism in the Jordan Valley for Europeans, and to enhance religious pilgrimages for Muslims, Christians and Jews.[74] Palestinian entrepreneurs seem to prefer local ownership and management, rather than the introduction of multinational hotel conglomerates, but they would

139

need to refurbish and expand the hotels and enlarge the tour bus operations. Training would be needed in hotel management and restaurant service. Related services — restaurants, cafes, amusement parks, handicrafts, and banks — would need to be upgraded to handle the volume and provide a variety of activities. Some estimate that 1.5 million tourists could come yearly and that the tourist sector could grow from the current 3-4 percent of GNP to at least 15 percent.

- **Computers:** Palestinians could establish a specialized economic niche to serve local and regional needs, given their orientation toward intellectual capital. A firm in Gaza is already producing state-of-the-art software. Engineers from the diaspora have the requisite skills in R&D on computer software and hardware, and manufacturing firms could absorb a reasonable number of assembly-line workers.

- **Communications and Journalism:** Palestinians could use their advanced educational skills and concern for freedom of speech and democratization to establish a communications hub for the region. Specialized journals in sciences, medicine, and agriculture could be published as well as literary and political magazines.

- **Banking services:** Based on Palestinian expertise from the diaspora, and intensive training and institution building during the interim period, Palestinians could provide banking and financial services for the wider Middle East, as Beirut did in the past.

- **Medical services:** The provision of specialized health care — perhaps for children, eye diseases, or heart surgery — would serve local and regional needs, utilizing both the basic medical infrastructure available in the OT and the skills of diaspora Palestinians, particularly from Kuwait. Substantial investment in facilities would be required. In time, Palestinian health services might become the premier provider of medical care in the Arab world and could provide training in health care throughout the region.

- **Regional educational center:** Arab students could come to the West Bank and Gaza, rather than Europe or the US, for quality university education in an atmosphere of academic freedom.

140

• **Scientific research:** Bioagricultural and biochemical research (such as tissue culture and enzymes) would build on the scientific and technical skills of the Palestinians and serve both international and local interests. It would require strict quality control and the establishment of specialized scientific research institutes.

The Role of the PLO

The economic and financial role of PLO institutions would be transformed in a final settlement. Planning and fundraising institutions would merge into the Palestinian or Palestinian-Jordanian governing bodies. Nonetheless, Palestinian diplomatic institutions would still play an important role for Palestinians who remain in the diaspora; their degree of coordination with Jordanian diplomatic missions would depend on the form of government established. Four possible roles include:

• Channel welfare assistance and some economic aid to Palestinian refugees who remain in Lebanon, Syria, Kuwait, and Egypt.

• Coordinate the payment of compensation funds to 1948 refugees living in the diaspora.

• Help to channel and collect funds from Palestinian businessmen and professionals living in the diaspora intended to build Palestinian economic and social institutions.

• Serve as trade and labor bureaus in order to promote economic relations in the Arab world and internationally.

External Aid

Even though Palestinians want to avoid permanent dependency on aid from foreign sources, they talk of the need for a Middle Eastern Marshall Plan, which would provide critical resources for their own people and help to ensure the realization of a regional economic community.[75] While the US, Europe, Japan and the oil-producing Arab states may not have the capacity to provide the level of investment and aid which is sought, Gottlieb points out that "the US and the EC have the means to reinforce the commonality of economic interests between Israel and its Arab neighbors... The US-Israeli Free Trade Agreement could be extended to the whole of a nascent Middle East common market community while the EC [could] enter into a generous agreement of association with it."[76]

The best procedure might be to establish a comprehensive fund and plan, both for the payment of compensation to Israelis and Palestinians and for the judicious investment in the Palestinian infrastructure and economy. That would minimize the risk of duplication and competition and ensure that funds were channeled to high priority projects. Given that Palestinian needs will be much higher than available funds, such coordination would seem essential.

Trade Arrangements for Palestinians and Israelis

Trade, tariff and currency agreements would need to be finalized between Israel and the PSA. Considerable coordination of monetary policy, foreign exchange management, tariffs and taxes would remain essential, so long as no barriers to trade are erected. Additional agreements would be needed between Israel and Arab states and (if the Palestinians gain a fully independent state) between the Palestinian state and Arab governments. Palestinians might want some protection for their agricultural and industrial goods from competition with Israel, but they would also want access to the Israeli market for those goods. Therefore, reciprocal accords would serve the interests of both parties. Agreements would also be needed concerning the employment of Palestinians inside Israel and the possible establishment of joint ventures in trade, tourism, industry and agriculture.

The Palestinian state or federation with Jordan would want to have access to Arab markets and would therefore seek the reduction or elimination of trade and labor barriers. That would be particularly important because the domestic market in the Palestinian area would be too small to support a diversified economy ensuring satisfactory living standards.

The Arab economic boycott of Israel would be fully lifted by the final stage, trade agreements would be implemented, and the sale of oil from Arab states to Israel initiated during the interim period would continue. Israeli banking, finance, computer, scientific and health services could attract clients in the Arab states. Israel would benefit from the expansion of tourism, and could undertake joint projects with Palestinian and Arab entrepreneurs. Joint Israeli-Jordanian tourism projects based in Eilat and Aqaba could be established as well as tour boats across the Dead Sea.[77] Those activities would provide strong economic incentives for Israel to carry out the political agreements and would create a visible public within Israel favoring cooperation with the Arab world. Ultimately, Israelis would gain the regional economic ties and collaboration to which they have long aspired and which would signal the normalization of their relations with their neighbors.

Finally, issues of compensating refugees would be resolved in the final stage following the interim period. Palestinian refugees who lost their property and bank accounts inside Israel in 1948 would need to receive adequate compensation in order to defuse their resentment and to reduce irredentist feelings. That compensation would enable refugees to construct housing and establish businesses in the Palestinian area or abroad. Jewish Israelis who fled Arab countries would also need to receive compensation for their lost property in order to rectify the damage done to them. A multilateral committee could be constituted to record and evaluate the amounts, based in part on longstanding UN records on the Palestinians and Israeli documents on Jewish claims. Such compensation would help stabilize and underscore the political resolution of the Israeli-Palestinian conflict.

Endnotes to Chapter III

1. Patrick Clawson and Howard Rosen, "The Economic Consequences of Peace for Israel, the Palestinians and Jordan," *Policy Paper* No. 25, The Washington Institute for Near East Policy, p.17. In June 1967, the combined GNP of the West Bank and Gaza Strip was only 2.6 percent of the Israeli GNP; A.M. Lesch in Lesch and Mark Tessler, *Israel, Egypt and the Palestinians* (Bloomington: Indiana University Press, 1989), p. 245 based on Meron Benvenisti, *The West Bank and Gaza* (Washington, D.C.: American Enterprise Institute, 1983), p. 53.

2. For details, including charts of the planning process and requirements for obtaining building permits, see Rami S. Abdulhadi, "Land Use Planning in the Occupied Palestinian Territories," *Journal of Palestine Studies*, XIX: 4 (summer 1990), pp. 46-63. Abdulhadi notes (pp. 54, 61-62) that, since 1982, Israel has prepared land use plans for nearly three hundred Palestinian villages, without any Palestinian input in their preparation. For example, eleven village plans approved in 1989 by the Higher Planning Council were based on plans prepared by its (all Israeli) Central Planning Department without any local input. Those eleven villages lacked elected councils that might have objected; in any event, appeal would be to the Higher Planning Council itself, which would be free to reject the complaints.

3. Figures from "US Loan Guarantees for Immigrant Absorption," GAO/NSIAD - 92 - 119, p. 19, fn 2. Raja Shehadeh, "The Changing Juridical Status of Palestinian Areas under Occupation," pp. 177-188

and Ibrahim Matar, "Israeli Settlements and Palestinian Rights," pp. 204-206 in Aruri; and Shalev, pp. 99, 105-6. The GAO report states that Israeli settlements are located on "a fraction" of the seized land. Lesch in Lesch and Tessler, p. 242, cites 1982 figures from Meron Benvenisti that the Israeli government controlled 28,450 acres in the Gaza Strip, 30 percent of its land mass, and used that almost entirely for settlements and their special access roads; only 475 acres were reserved for army bases. Shamgar, Appendix C, provides the text for military order no. 58 concerning "abandoned" (i.e. absentee) property.

4. Gershon Baskin, "Israel Puts the Squeeze on West Bank Water Resources," *Challenge*, 2:1 (January-March 1991), pp. 16-17; *Middle East International*, 26 May 1989, p. 16; Jeffrey D. Dillman, "Water Rights in the Occupied Territories," *Journal of Palestine Studies*, XIX: 1 (autumn 1989), pp. 46-71. Although many municipalities control the supply of water within their boundaries, the military government must approve all municipal plans, budgets and rates (Drori in Shamgar, pp. 245, 253); Drori notes that the Internal Affairs Officer in the military government controls the nominally-local water authority for Bethlehem, Beit Jala and Beit Sahour. In any case, once the Israeli military took over most municipalities in 1982, the value to Palestinians of municipal control over water diminished.

5. A leading Israeli expert at a meeting of the water committee of the Israel Palestine Center for Research and Information (ICPRI) in 1991 stated that 85-90 percent of the water from the mountain aquifer (300-350 mcm yearly) is used by Israeli wells in the pre-1967 area. Valuable essays on Israeli and Palestinian water use are contained in *Water: Conflict or Cooperation*, ed. Gershon Baskin (IPCRI: I:2, May 1992), especially by Hillel Shuval, Nader al-Khatib and Isam R. Shawwa. See also Shalev, pp. 137-8.

6. Detailed figures are provided by Isam R. Shawwa, "The Water Situation in the Gaza Strip," in Baskin, pp. 16-20. See also A. M. Lesch, "Gaza: Life under Occupation," in Lesch and Tessler, p. 248. *Jerusalem Post* (International Edition) 18 January 1992 reported that, in response to the emergency conditions, Mekorot Water Company completed laying a 30-km long water line to supply 20 mcm daily from the National Water Carrier to the Gaza Strip. It was unclear whether this pipeline would serve settlements or Palestinian residents.

7. Settlements receive most of their water from the Israeli National Water Carrier: data on the share of water taken from the Strip is not available since statistics on water use are highly classified. Dillman, p. 53, contrasts two credible researchers: David Kahan estimates that settlers have 2,667 cm yearly per capita or 5 mcm yearly; whereas Sara Roy estimates that settlers use at least 14,200 cm per capita and 30-60 mcm yearly. This report bases its comparison on the lower figure.

8. For details on electricity, see *Masterplanning the State of Palestine* (Center for Engineering and Planning, Ramallah), pp. 79-83.

9. Dillman, p. 55. For 1988 figures on agricultural output in the OT, see PASSIA, pp. 44-45. Citrus (oranges, lemon, tangerines, and grapefruit) cover 17,500 acres in the Strip, i.e. half its agricultural output, 70 percent of agricultural exports, a third of the cultivated area, and 55 percent of the value of agricultural production. The peak yield (1975-76) was 237,000 tons or 1.3 tons per acre. As trees aged or were uprooted, the quantity and quality declined. By 1982-83, yield was 153,000 tons or 0.87 tons per acre. Lesch in Lesch and Tessler, p. 247. Ruth Klinov notes that Israelis also need a permit in order to plant vegetables and fruit and are fined heavily if they violate the order.

10. Jad Isaac told the author that the West Bank had nine experimental stations until 1973, but now has no government agricultural research project. He cited figures from David Kahan (1987) that 464 Palestinians worked in the agricultural extension department of the military government in 1975, but only 219 in 1987; funds were cut from an estimated $59,000 for agricultural research in 1972 to $14,600 in 1981.

11. Statistical Abstract of Israel (1988), cited in PASSIA, p. 39.

12. Specifics on factories and fishing from Lesch in Lesch and Tessler, pp. 246-248, and mimeographed essay by Abd al-Rahman Abu Arafa on "Development of the Palestinian Agricultural Marketing Sector" (Arabic).

13. Clawson and Rosen, p. 13. See also PASSIA, p. 43, for specific dollar figures on imports and exports in 1988, based on the *Statistical Abstract of Israel*. Statistics for Gaza in Lesch and Tessler, p. 245, include a reference from 1978 to two thirds of Gaza exports going to Israel (some for reexport), 26 percent to Jordan and 7 percent elsewhere; 91 percent of imports came from Israel and none came from Jordan.

14. Abu Arafa, "Development of the Palestinian Agricultural Market Sector."

15. Matteson in Gubser, p. 13.

16. Ruth Klinov provided figures for both the West Bank and Gaza Strip: in 1989 105,000 worked in Israel and 108,000 in 1990; whereas January-June 1991 only 80-90,000 worked in Israel. However, 106,000 worked in Israel July-September 1991 (the third quarter), indicating a return to the pre-war level. Israeli sociologist Michael Shalev told the author on 18 March 1992 that the latter figure might be too high, since the official employment service listed 75,000 workers in November 1991 and severe restrictions were still placed on "black market" (unofficial) labor in Israel. That tallies with Gubser's report in fall 1991 (p. 9) that, whereas 100,000 Gazans worked in Israel before the Gulf crisis, subsequently 55,000 received work permits and only 35,000 worked in Israel on a regular basis.

17. Comments by Raja Shehadeh and Ibrahim Matar, January 1992, and Osama Hamed, October 1991. See Sara Roy, "Development under Occupation: The Political Economy of U.S. Aid to the West Bank and Gaza Strip," *Arab Studies Quarterly* (13: 3&4, summer/fall 1991), pp. 65, 76, 78.

18. Clawson and Rosen, p. 42, and comments by Dr. Osama Hamed. See his unpublished research paper with Radwan A. Sha'aban, "Economic Integration and Israeli Occupation of the West Bank and Gaza," presented at the Conference on Economic Units, Institute for Social and Economic Policy in the Middle East, Kennedy School, Harvard University, 14-16 November 1991.

19. Roy, 81. See also the discussion on development options in *Tanmiya* (Geneva: The Welfare Association), No. 25, December 1991, pp. 6-7.

20. Samir Hulaileh, "The Gulf Crisis and the Palestinian Economy," in *Palestinian Assessment of the Gulf War and Its Aftermath*, PASSIA, 1991, pp. 39-40. Glenn Robinson, in his forthcoming article in IJMES, "The Role of the Professional Middle Class in the Mobilization of Palestinian Society: The Medical and Agricultural Committees," cites Israeli statistics for FY 1987-88 that indicate that the value of West Bank products increased significantly: 26 percent for milk, 22 percent for livestock, and 20 percent for eggs. In the Gaza Strip, the value of fish increased 76 percent, milk 28 percent and vegetables 25 percent. The Nablus area nearly doubled its vegetable and citrus area in 1988-9. Israeli vegetables and fruit had been two thirds of OT consumption before the intifada, but dropped to 10 percent.

21. Olive trees have been frequently uprooted by the Israeli army and settlers as a punitive measure. From December 1987 through September 1991, more than 123,000 trees were uprooted and 379,000 dunums of land confiscated. (One dunum is approximately a quarter acre.) *Gulf War Aftermath*, monograph by the Human Rights Research Foundation, December 1991, p. 13.

22. Matteson in Gubser, pp. 13-14.

23. Robinson, forthcoming article.

24. Information on the organizations comes from *Tanmiya*, # 25, pp. 1-3.

25. Directed by Dr. Jad Isaac, who was detained for six months for distributing the above-mentioned seeds, ARIJ is creating a bibliography on agricultural and water resources and working to foster awareness of ecological issues. West Bank universities have sponsored conferences on development issues: in July 1991, for example, Najah University hosted a conference on water and sanitation and Hebron University held a workshop on livestock production.

26. Information from Ibrahim Matar and Lance Matteson, ANERA, January 1992.

27. Elections were held in in Gaza, Hebron, Jericho, Ramallah, Nablus, and East Jerusalem, but were canceled in Jenin and Qalqilya when Israel barred certain candidates. *Al-Fajr*, 7 October 1991, p. 12 notes that membership in the Jerusalem chamber of commerce was extended to owners of service-oriented businesses: restaurants, cafes, barbershops, and laundromats. Palestinians boycotted elections for a new body in Bethlehem, called the Chamber of Industry, which Israel sought to establish. They objected to Israel's defining the status of the chamber and setting the criteria for membership. No one stood for election and the poll was cancelled.

28. See Roy, "Development," pp. 65-79.

29. Figures on US aid from Peter Gubser (ANERA), 1 June 1992. Other trade and aid data from PASSIA, pp. 46-47. A large number of European private agencies provide assistance to the OT, including Oxfam, Caritas, NOVIB (Netherlands), and church-affiliated charities such as Lutheran World Federation and the Pontifical Mission (Vatican); see PASSIA, pp. 49-50.

30. The head of the Israeli civil administration reportedly told the Tulkarm Chamber of Commerce, Industry and Agriculture, in a meeting on 24 September 1991, that he might allow three-month travel permits, through the Chamber, to merchants and their cars. He added that he would cancel car taxes on 1 April 1992 and would study the issue of car insurance fees. He also hinted that applications for family reunion, submitted through the Chamber, might be granted to persons who had capital to invest in local enterprises. *Al-Fajr*, 30 September 1991, p. 3.

31. Recommended in the Ezra Sadan Commission report, commissioned by the Defense Ministry to propose changes in the economy of the Gaza Strip; cited in Daoud Kuttab, "In the Aftermath of War," *Journal of Palestine Studies*, XX:4 (summer 1991), pp. 117-118.

32. Ahmad Abu Ala, director of the PLO's economic department, stated that he anticipates $13 billion financing from the world community and Arab and Palestinian businessmen during the interim period. Interview in *Middle East Times*, 5 November 1991, p. 6.

33. For information on the Palestine National Fund, see chapter by Adam Zagorin in Augustus Richard Norton and Martin H. Greenberg, eds. *The International Relations of the Palestine Liberation Organization* (Carbondale: Southern Illinois University Press, 1989).

34. Roy, "Development," pp. 84-85, lists seven ways in which the USAID program could be changed in order to improve its effectiveness and relevance, the first of which is to eliminate Israeli government control over project clearance. She also outlines seven program guidelines that international donors should follow in order to promote genuine development in the OT. Roy's suggestions complement the emphases in this essay.

35. Stressed by Lance Matteson of ANERA. Abu Arafa, in his study on agricultural marketing, emphasizes the lack of planning, weakness of central wholesale markets owned and managed by municipalities, and problems of transport as key problems, in addition to the restrictions placed by Israel and Jordan on marketing produce.

36. Some studies are already underway, for example an UNCTAD study under UNDP auspices on economic development; an AID study of the 7-8 main economic sectors; an ANERA funded study of future infrastructure over 5-10 years, including roads and housing; and a Norwegian trade union movement study of living conditions in 1000 Gaza households, for which the interviews were completed in fall 1991.

37. ANERA is seeking to establish a bank to offer medium level loans, potentially in conjunction with an international financial institution and/or a branch of a Jordan-based bank.

38. Israel has developed its own plans already, for example the chief water engineer of Tahal wrote a classified report for the Jaffee Center at Tel Aviv University outlining a regional water plan in the event of peace. The Center may publish parts of that report.

39. Anthony Lewis (*The New York Times*, 23 January 1992) quoted leading Israeli industrialists: Dov Frohman of the microchip firm Intel Israel said, "The problem is political and economic instability. Why would a business want to go to an unstable place?" and added "Peace is the great thing. I don't think we can get accelerated growth unless we solve the problem." Aharon Dovrat, founder of Clal, the largest private conglomerate, said "Peace is a precondition to attract investment on any scale. It is our only hope... If Israel had had peace for the last ten years, it would be approaching Switzerland. People won't send their money to a country that is full of unrest. The idea of attracting investment and at the same time building settlements on occupied land is completely crazy."

40. Kuttab, p. 117. The Sadan Report on the economy of Gaza recommended that the government open industrial parks within the Strip where new industries would receive a three-year waiver in taxes and that Gaza products be sold freely in Israel. The report assumed that the Israeli and Gaza economies would remain connected on a longterm basis. Its proposals to foster industrialization would ease the unemployment problem inside the Strip, help its economy shift away from agriculture, and enable Israel to limit the presence of Palestinian workers inside Israel.

41. IPCRI, through its economists and industrialists forum, is encouraging an Israeli and a Palestinian economist to write a ten-year projection of the economic implications of a Palestinian-Israeli peace; another team is looking at economic policy for the OT, including areas for potential economic cooperation.

42. Clawson and Rosen argue that banks, credit unions, local savings societies, and mutual investment funds are needed urgently in the OT (p.71). They propose that a neutral body, staffed by the IMF with the approval of the Israeli and Jordanian central banks, be established as a regulatory agency for financial transactions (p. 72).

43. Clawson and Rosen analyze four scenarios: economic autarchy for Israel, the Palestinian OT and Jordan; a return to the pre-1967 patterns, with Israel closed off but Palestine and Jordan linked; the establishment of a trade zone (but not free labor flows) among the three areas; and a Benelux arrangement, with free movement of goods and labor among the three. They conclude that autarchy would result in the most severe adjustment problems for the Palestinians, whereas adjustment would be minimal for Israel and Jordan. A return to the pre-1967 pattern would benefit the Palestinians if it reopened trade and labor flows to Jordan and the Arab world. A free trade zone would leave the Palestinians vulnerable to Israeli and Jordanian protectionism and would not solve the Palestinians' labor problems. Benelux would be best for the Palestinians, since labor and trade could expand toward both Jordan and Israel; Israel would also benefit from a Benelux arrangement, particularly in trade, whereas Jordan would be wary about the competition that such an arrangement would entail.

44. Adel Samara, among others, points out that labor unions have subordinated worker interests to the national struggle. Unions, for example, have stopped strikes in order to protect national unity. Conversely, splits in the union ranks have resulted from political differences rather than from class or union issues, according to Samara. Thus, the unions have been ineffective in improving working conditions, hours and wages and have failed to even establish a minimum wage level for factories in the OT. *News from Within*, 5 December 1991, pp. 14-15. Hiltermann, *Behind the Intifada*, argues that unions have effected some improvements despite those difficulties.

45. The following paragraphs are based largely on Klinov.

46. The Palestinian economist Osama Hamed suggested to the author that the simplest scheme would involve splitting, at the end of each year, total imports and total receipts from tariffs in proportion to the share of Israel and the OT. The issue of tax collection for Israeli settlements is thorny politically within Israel: in the likely event that their taxes would not go to the ISGA coffers, would they continue to have preferential tax and mortgage rates status vis-a-vis other Israelis?

47. A preliminary effort at planning the infrastructure and economy, including transport, communications and public utilities, has been published by the Center for Engineering and Planning, *Masterplanning the State of Palestine: Suggested Guidelines for Comprehensive Development* (Ramallah, March 1992).

48. Janet L. Abu-Lughod, "The Demographic Consequences of the Occupation," in Aruri, p. 408, notes that 20.8 percent of Palestinian men in Kuwait held professional or technical jobs, according to the 1975 census, and 37 percent of the Palestinians in Saudi Arabia held such high level jobs in 1974. In contrast, only 6.2 percent in the West Bank and 5.1 percent in the Gaza Strip held professional or technical jobs in 1977, according to the *Statistical Abstract of Israel, 1978.* Israeli statistics for 1989 showed a drop for the West Bank to 5.3 percent of the work force and a static 5.1 percent for Gaza; as cited in PASSIA, p. 41.

49. Those ideas are detailed in Abu Arafa.

50. Clawson and Rosen, footnote p. 45, maintain that local savings would amount only to $220 million yearly and therefore private foreign capital would be an important supplement. However, they believe that such capital would only enter the OT if the political situation were settled (p. 60). They argue that George Abed's assumption that $11.5 billion would be available over five years from domestic savings and private foreign capital is "implausible" (p. 45).

51. Clawson and Rosen, pp. 51, 54. They strongly criticize Israel's "misguided mercantilism" (p. 70) toward the OT as well as Israel's protection of its monopolies.

52. Abu Arafa provides detailed charts and statistics on all of those potential industries, based on local agriculture.

53. For details on quarrying, see *Masterplanning the State of Palestine,* pp. 44-45, 61, 146.

54. For example, Abd al-Latif Gheith commented: "If there were a plan for autonomy that included control over lands and water, where the source of authority would be Palestinian, and which would be defined as an interim stage on the way to statehood — even if this stage would take five or ten years", then I could consider it. Interview in *News from Within,* VII:12, 5 December 1991, p. 4.

55. Clawson and Rosen, pp. 69-70. Future energy needs are also discussed in *Masterplanning,* p. 173-4.

56. Shuval, "Approaches to Finding an Equitable Solution to the Water Resources Problems Shared by Israel and the Palestinians Over the Use of the Mountain Aquifer," in Baskin, pp. 40-42. Shuval describes Israel, the OT and Jordan as "water stress zones" since less than 500 cm per capita yearly is available: Israel uses 375 cm per capita yearly, the OT 165 cm and Jordan 260 cm. A 30 year plan must take into account the doubling of Israelis and Palestinians to 14 million (10 million Israelis and 4 million Palestinians).

57. Nader al-Khatib, "Palestinian Water Rights," in Baskin, p. 13. Dillman (pp. 47, 57) says 125 mcm water would be available from east of the watershed, of which 30 mcm is now used by Israeli settlements in the Jordan Valley. He also discusses the problems posed by settlement wells

that dry up Palestinian water sources and notes that, whereas only five permits have been granted to Palestinians for new wells since 1967, at least 55 permits have been given to settlements (35-40 in the over-pumped Gaza Strip). See also, Miriam Lowi, "West Bank Water Resources and the Resolution of Conflict in the Middle East," Occasional Paper No. 1 of the Project on Environmental Change and Acute Conflict, American Academy of Arts and Sciences, forthcoming.

58. Suggested in *Masterplanning the State of Palestine*, p. 41.

59. At present, only a third of West Bank villages have piped water; 50-60 percent of urban areas have sewage networks, which are poorly maintained. Waste water flows untreated from the OT towns into open channels for use in irrigation, causing serious health problems and contaminating agricultural soils. The Gaza Strip produces 35 mcm sewage water yearly. UNRWA and the Bir Zeit University Community Health Unit have studied the impact of environmental contamination from sewage in Gaza: the study found that half the population had parasites from feces. Shawa in Baskin, pp. 20-21; *Tanmiya*, December 1991, p. 2.

60. Shawa in Baskin, p. 21. The Gaza municipality commissioned the plan in 1977 and raised funds in Abu Dhabi. Construction began in 1985 and the system is expected to inject at least 1.5 mcm yearly into the aquifer.

61. A preliminary study by the UNDP in 1990 indicated that, in the first stage, a seawater desalinization plant could generate 50 megawatts of electric power and produce 18 mcm fresh water yearly with a $180 million capital investment; each cubic meter of water would cost $1.00. A study by Israel Desalination Engineers, Ltd., in 1990 concluded that the same amount of electricity and water could be produced at half the cost, 48 cents per cm. Shuval assumes that the $1 figure is likely and that desalinating brackish water would cost half as much. See Shawwa (pp. 21-24) and Shuval (pp. 47-48) in Baskin.

62. Comments to the author, 16 April 1992 and Thomas Naff, "The Jordan Basin: Political, Economic and Institutional Issues," proceedings of the World Bank Conference on World Water Problems, June 1991. Naff as well as Clawson and Rosen argue that Israeli and Jordanian subsidies to farmers in the form of cheap water are the main cause of wasteful overuse of water. The latter argue (p. 66) that raising the price of agricultural water, combined with administrative regulations to eliminate water-hogging crops such as cotton, would be the most vital components of a revised Israeli water policy. Much of the information in this section comes from confidential Israeli-Palestinian discussions under the auspices of IPCRI in 1991.

63. Naff; Shuval in Baskin. The Jordan government stresses the need for a regional water sharing formula to avert future conflicts resulting from attempts to control water supplies. Regional cooperation in the wake of an Arab-Israeli peace, the government argues, would lead not only to

completing Unity Dam but also to internationally-supported regional efforts to build a series of small dams in the Jordan basin, construct water treatment plants, and utilize brackish water for agriculture. Those projects would enhance economic life and deepen the foundations for regional peace and security. *Jordan: Issues and Perspectives*, October/November 1991, p. 3.

64. Suggested by Naff, 16 April 1992.

65. Shuval in Baskin, p. 46; Thomas Naff, "Israel and the Waters of South Lebanon," unpublished paper for the Center for Lebanese Studies, Oxford, October 1991.

66. Shuval in Baskin, pp. 46-48.

67. Shuval in Baskin, pp. 46, 48.

68. Suggested by Roy, p. 85.

69. Naff, pp. 41-42.

70. Zeev Hirsch completed a feasibility study for a deep water port in Gaza that would cost at least $500 million. In a discussion of the report at IPCRI, Palestinian economists preferred to invest in commerce and other aspects of the Gaza infrastructure and rely, at least initially, on Israeli ports.

71. *Masterplanning* also suggests that local airports could be built near Jenin and Jericho, p. 74.

72. Palestinian-Israeli joint statement in *al-Fajr*, 23 September 1991.

73. Such institutionalized networks are viewed as urgent by Naff, Shuval and Khatib, in their essays cited above.

74. Comments by Bruce Stanley of AMIDEAST and Jad Isaac, January 1992. The concept of East Jerusalem and the West Bank as a cultural and tourist center was advanced by Walid Khalidi, 1978, p. 710.

75. Gottlieb, 1989, p. 117 quotes Arafat on that issue. Moughrabi, p. 40, also mentions that and speaks of the Palestinians needing at least $1 billion for each of the five years of autonomy.

76. Gottlieb, p. 117.

77. Alouph Hareven mentioned those projects to the author as ones that some Israeli entrepreneurs are already considering, 7 January 1992.

Executive Summary

The onset of Israeli-Palestinian negotiations in 1991 has introduced the possibility of mutually-agreed substantive changes to decades of bitter Palestinian-Israeli relations. An accord on interim self-rule for Palestinians living on the West Bank and Gaza could greatly alter current relations between the two communities by sharply reducing the potentials for violence and easing the tensions of daily living for Israelis and Palestinians. This report specifies three arenas in which agreement will be vital:

• The civil-political arena: governing and administrative institutions and functions need to be turned over gradually to Palestinian control, ensuring the smooth operation of essential services and the establishment of mechanisms of planning by Palestinian authorities that are accountable to the public in the West Bank and Gaza;

• Security: Israel's external and internal security requirements must be met while simultaneously meeting the need to reduce Palestinian insecurity and enabling the governing authority to maintain civic order; these bilateral arrangements must be coupled with the development of a regional security system;

• Economic and resource issues: self-government will require Palestinian responsibility for, and control of, policy and planning as well as daily administration; substantive shifts in economic and resource practices will be required; Israel's needs will be met by joint monitoring bodies and enhancement of Israeli trade and contacts with the Arab world.

Civic and Political Institutions

At present, all substantive power is in the hands of the military government and its civil administration. Palestinians have little or no say in political and administrative policies and practices that affect their lives; they are prohibited from exercising meaningful political, press and institutional freedom.

During negotiations, important steps can be taken by the Israelis to remove many of the restrictions on civic, educational and political life. Elections to municipal and village councils could be held as a means to support negotiations and expand the popular base of the anticipated Interim Self-Governing Authority (ISGA). Palestinians and Israelis could expand joint consultations and projects dealing with critical economic, cultural and political issues. From outside the region, the PLO could provide technical support for the negotiating process, and the United States and European Community could encourage the peace process in tangible ways, notably by encouraging Palestinian institution-building and ensuring that foreign donors work directly with Palestinian organizations.

During the specified interim period, Palestinian authority would be derived from the negotiated agreement. The ISGA would take responsibility for normal civic functions, e.g.: formulate public policy, levy taxes and regulate finances, control police and local security (in coordination with Israel at the regional level), operate educational, health and other vital services, and exercise joint control over land and water resources. Personal and territorial self-rule are seen as inextricably intertwined: the people are not separate from the land. While current negotiating parameters exclude East Jerusalem from being formally included in the ISGA, it seems important that its Palestinian residents be eligible to work and vote for candidates in the ISGA.

A phased process would remove the current barriers to civic life in the territories and create the structures of Palestinian self-government. Two sets of elections would be needed early in the interim period: to ratify the negotiated agreement and to elect the ISGA.

The executive council of the ISGA with policymaking and financial authority would establish a civil service commission, a special body to revise the legal system, and departments that would conduct the daily operations of the society. Current administrative structures might be incorporated into their frameworks. Some of the current non-governmental organizations such as the coordinating councils for agriculture, education, housing, and industry, would be absorbed into the ISGA administration, whereas others would remain independent, as part of the Palestinian voluntary association network. District level administration (abolished in 1967) would be re-established and municipal and village councils reconstituted and elections held. Aid to the ISGA and local authorities from the international community would be especially needed in management, planning and technical fields. Joint research with Israelis designed to facilitate educational and cultural contact and to address outstanding problems such as water and Jerusalem would also be vital during the interim period.

In the long term, the Palestinian sovereign authority (PSA) would mean either an independent state or a confederation with Jordan. The PSA would have international standing and its own representation in international bodies. The phased return of Palestinians from the diaspora would be arranged and the legal status of those who remain abroad would be regularized in their host countries. The controversial issues of Jerusalem and Israeli settlements would be resolved at this time. In the context of a peace accord and open borders, creative means to share Jerusalem between the Israelis and Palestinians could be devised; Israelis who wish to remain in settlements would have the option to do so under the jurisdiction of the PSA, probably with the status of foreign residents.

External and Internal Security

Israelis and Palestinians both place strong emphasis on the safety and survival of their communities in the face of external threat and internal violence. Each believes that its security is undermined by the other's beliefs and actions. Their concerns are asymmetrical: Israelis focus primarily on regional security whereas the Palestinians are preoccupied with communal insecurity caused by Israel's military occupation and by their vulnerable status in Arab countries. The mutuality of their needs must be recognized. Moreover, for Israel to consider withdrawing militarily from the Occupied Territories, its security at the regional level needs to be assured.

During negotiations, Israel's primary emphasis will be with regional security concerns. Bilateral negotiations with Syria, Lebanon and Jordan are a vital component of that process, complemented by multilateral talks on regional arms control and limits on weapons of mass destruction and long-range missiles.

Successful steps in the negotiations would positively affect Israel's approach to security in the territories and enable its military command to consider a gradual but substantial withdrawal from the heart of the West Bank; the occupied territories would remain demilitarized.

Palestinians could act to reduce violence by seeking to stop armed attacks against Israelis or other Palestinians and reaffirming their opposition to terrorism. Palestinian leaders might also declare explicitly that the future Palestinian state would be demilitarized and committed to peaceful relations with its neighbors. Such measures would seek to alleviate the existential fears of Israelis and promote a climate conducive to an accord.

During the interim period vis-a-vis an Israeli-Jordanian security regime, Israeli forces would withdraw on a phased basis from their bases in the center of the Occupied Territories and redeploy to sites in the Jordan Valley. Israel would continue to control the bridge and border crossings to Jordan and Egypt. Israel would also continue to maintain and guard its early warning stations on the ridges overlooking the Jordan Valley, its air force would continue to overfly the territories, and its navy would patrol the coast off Gaza. An Israeli-Palestinian-Jordanian commission would monitor security arrangements and handle violations.

The Palestinian ISGA would gradually assume responsibility for internal security in the West Bank and Gaza. A Palestinian police force and court system would be reconstructed and strengthened to maintain order as the Israeli armed forces withdrew. Special Israeli-Palestinian police patrols would be constituted to maintain security on the highways and guard vital installations. Reciprocal security arrangements would be specified to handle potential violence between Palestinians and Israelis, perhaps by establishing a joint crisis monitoring center. A comprehensive security plan would permit both peoples to travel freely, but would prevent additional Israeli settlement in the territories and the return of Palestinians from exile during the interim period.

In the long term, the linked peace and security accords would be fully implemented, with borders open for trade and tourism. A trilateral security regime for Israel-Palestine-Jordan would consist of full diplomatic relations, a non-aggression pact, mutually agreed security measures along the borders, participation in regional and international arms control agreements, and continued demilitarization of the Palestinian Sovereign Authority.

Economic and Resource Issues

The economic relationships between Israel and the OT would be recast to promote mutual benefits. There will be some asymmetries: Palestinians would gain control over their resources and livelihood, Israel could lose what had seemed to be guaranteed markets and easy access to a large labor pool. Israel would, however, realize new gains with the Arab world in both commerce and potentially increased access to water and electricity.

During the negotiations, Israel could take measures to help promote a constructive political atmosphere by, for example, lifting travel restrictions, stopping tax raids, easing access for Palestinian goods into Israel and abroad, adopting a liberal licensing policy toward businesses, enabling municipalities to engage in planning, reopening banks, restructuring taxes, renewing land registration, and undertaking joint assessments of water use. Palestinians would be able to accelerate their efforts to set up credit institutions, improve technical research and outreach, and coordinate these activities. International agencies would promote market surveys, designs for the ISGA infrastructure, development of technical and managerial skills, and planning for credit institutions.

For its part, Jordan would lift its ban on importing manufactured goods from the West Bank and Gaza, the Gulf states would begin to negotiate the sale of oil to Israel, and regional discussions on marketing and water resource planning would be initiated. These steps would enhance Israel's confidence that it would gain economically from an accord. In the interim phase, Israel would remove barriers that limit Palestinian trade, credit, and population movement. The ISGA would have financial and monetary authority, including the right to levy taxes and negotiate external grants and loans, although fiscal and monetary policy would be coordinated with Israel. The ISGA would engage in long-term economic planning, particularly to enhance the basic infrastructure and expand housing. Private investors would seek to expand light industries in a wide variety of fields, including pharmaceuticals, clothing, shoemaking, and agricultural and fishing industries. External agencies would provide direct grants for large-scale infrastructure projects, for onetime start-up capital for selected businesses, and for pilot projects; loans would be made available through indigenous credit institutions as well as continued technical assistance and training.

Access to natural resources would be essential for the ISGA. A joint Israeli-Palestinian commission would examine land use, and enable the ISGA to have access to public and absentee land. Initially, a joint board would also handle electricity; the ISGA would progressively gain authority over electricity and groundwater in the OT, with a joint authority to determine mutual needs and regulate the level of pumping in both Israel and the OT.

Regional water plans would be an important component of the bilateral and multilateral accords. The opportunity to increase access to water would serve as one of the inducements for Israel to negotiate security accords with its neighbors. Projects to be given high priority would include the Unity Dam on the Yarmouk River involving Jordan, Syria and Israel, pipelines for water from the Litani River in Lebanon and from Turkey or Egypt, and a joint Jordan-Israel desalinization plant in Eilat/Aqaba.

During the interim period Israel would begin to purchase oil from the Gulf, as the Arab economic boycott ended. External agencies would have important roles in promoting the regional water projects and encouraging trade ties.

For the long term, the PSA would need to complete large scale infrastructure projects, in part to handle returnees from the diaspora. An integrated economic plan would be required for the Jordan Valley, north-south roads would be completed, the Gaza port overhauled, and the Qalandiya airport refurbished for international traffic. Waste water and desalination projects would be completed. Key economic areas would be enhanced, so that the PSA could serve as a regional center for tourism, education, medicine, communications, and scientific research. Trade, tariff and currency arrangements would be finalized between Israel and the PSA, with considerable coordination remaining necessary so long as trade and labor flows are open to both parties.

The PLO, whose structures would merge into Palestine/Jordan's diplomatic missions, would continue to assist Palestinians remaining in the diaspora, handle the payment of compensation funds to those refugees, and manage trade and labor bureaus. Similarly, Jews who lost property in Arab states would receive compensation, complementing the restitution of Palestinian property losses.

In sum, the dynamics of the Israeli-Palestinian peace process in the summer of 1992 suggest new and unanticipated opportunities for improving the relations between the two peoples, and it is with that goal in mind that the recommendations in this report are offered.

About the Authors

Jeffrey Boutwell is Associate Executive Officer at the American Academy of Arts and Sciences and director of the Academy's program on international security studies. He worked on the National Security Council staff during the Carter Administration and is the author of *The German Nuclear Dilemma* (Cornell University Press, 1990).

Naomi Chazan is a professor of political science and African Studies at the Hebrew University of Jerusalem, where she also is Chairperson of the Harry S Truman Institute for the Advancement of Peace. She is the author of several books and numerous articles on African political development, comparative politics and the Arab/Israeli confict. Among her most recent publications are *Irredentism and International Politics* (1991) and "Negotiating the Non-Negotiable: Jerusalem in the Framework of an Israeli-Palestinian Settlement," *Emerging Issues* Occasional Paper No. 7 (American Academy of Arts and Sciences, March 1991).

Mahdi Abdul Hadi is a political scientist and the President of PASSIA (The Palestinian Academic Society for the Study of International Affairs) which he founded in 1987. In 1984-85 he was a fellow at the Center for International Affairs at Harvard University. From 1985-86 he was special adviser to the Ministry of Occupied Land Affairs in Amman. Dr. Abdul Hadi is the author of several publications.

Ruth Klinov is an associate professor of economics at Hebrew University in Jerusalem. She specializes in labor markets, education, and social safety-net issues.

Ann Lesch is professor of political science and associate director of the Center for Arab and Islamic Studies at Villanova University. She is a member of the board for Middle East Watch and *Middle East Report*, and clerk of the Middle East Program Committee of the American Friends Service Committee. She was co-author with Mark Tessler of *Israel, Egypt and the Palestinians* (Indiana University Press, 1989).

Everett Mendelsohn is professor of the history of science at Harvard University, a Fellow of the American Academy of Arts and Sciences, and co-chair of its Committee on Middle East Security

Studies. He is the author of *A Compassionate Peace: A Future for Israel, Palestine, and the Middle East* (Hill & Wang, 1989).

Fouad Moughrabi is a professor of political science at University of Tennessee in Chattanooga, and a writer and lecturer in Middle East affairs. He is co-author of *Public Opinion and the Palestine Question* (St. Martin's Press, 1987).

Salim Tamari is associate professor of sociology at Bir Zeit University. He holds a Ph.D. from Manchester University, England. He is editor of the Bir Zeit University Social Science Review, *Afaq Filistiniyya* and associate editor at *Middle East Report* in Washington, DC. He is a member of the Steering Committee of the Multilateral Middle East Peace Negotiations and a member of the Working Group on Refugees for MMEPN.

Shibley Telhami is associate professor of government at Cornell University and served as a Council on Foreign Relations Fellow advising the United States Mission at the United Nations during the Gulf Crisis. He also served as adviser to Representative Lee H. Hamilton, Chairman of the House Subcommittee on Europe and the Middle East. He is the author of *Power and Leadership in International Bargaining: The Path to the Camp David Accords* (Columbia University Press, 1990) and numerous articles on international affairs.

Mark Tessler is professor of political science at the University of Wisconsin-Milwaukee. He has spent seven years in the Middle East, having attended universities in Israel and Tunisia and having conducted research in Israel, the West Bank, Tunisia and Morocco. He has published six books, the most recent being *Israel, Egypt and the Palestinians: From Camp David to Intifada*, which he co-authored with Ann Lesch.